The U.S. Congress

A Simulation for Students

The U.S. Congress

A Simulation for Students

LAUREN COHEN BELL
Randolph-Macon College

WADSWORTH
CENGAGE Learning·

Australia • Brazil • Japan • Korea • Mexico • Singapore • Spain • United Kingdom • United States

The U.S. Congress: A Simulation for Students
Lauren Cohen Bell

Political Science Executive Editor: David Tatom

Assistant Editor: Rebecca Green

Editorial Assistant: Reena Thomas

Technology Project Manager: Michelle Vardeman

Marketing Manager: Janise Fry

Marketing Assistant: Mary Ho

Advertising Project Manager: Kelly McAllister

Project Manager, Editorial Production: Ray Crawford

Art Director: Rob Hugel

Print/Media Buyer: Lisa Claudeanos

Permissions Editor: Stephanie Lee

Production Service: Scratchgravel Publishing Services

Copy Editor: Margaret C. Tropp

Cover Designer: Jeanette Barber

Cover Image: United States Capitol Building © Hisham F. Ibrahim/Getty Images; College Students Listening to Lecture © Royalty–Free/CORBIS

Compositor: Scratchgravel Publishing Services

For product information and technology assistance, contact us at
Cengage Learning Customer & Sales Support, 1-800-354-9706
For permission to use material from this text or product,
submit all requests online at **cengage.com/permissions**
Further permissions questions can be emailed to
permissionrequest@cengage.com

Library of Congress Control Number: 2003116811

ISBN-13: 978-0-534-63111-6

ISBN-10: 0-534-63111-8

Wadsworth
10 Davis Drive
Belmont, CA 94002-3098
USA

Cengage Learning is a leading provider of customized learning solutions with office locations around the globe, including Singapore, the United Kingdom, Australia, Mexico, Brazil, and Japan. Locate your local office at:
international.cengage.com/region

Cengage Learning products are represented in Canada by Nelson Education, Ltd.

For your course and learning solutions, visit **academic.cengage.com**

Purchase any of our products at your local college store or at our preferred online store **www.ichapters.com**

Printed in the United States of America
2 3 4 5 6   21 20 19 18 17

For my students, who make me excited to go to work every day;
for my husband, who makes me happy to come home each night;
and for my parents, who have been the greatest teachers I have ever known.

Contents

A Note to Instructors

Although the simulation described in Chapter Three prescribes a particular set and sequence of activities, this book is intended for individual instructors to adapt and change the simulation to work well within your particular courses. In the companion materials for this simulation, I offer suggestions about how to adapt this simulation to a variety of class settings and how to accomplish a variety of instructional objectives. For example, I describe several optional exercises that can be used—or not—depending on such factors as class size, achievement level, student interest, and your own desire. In addition, although I encourage students to be active in choosing their own leaders, selecting the members that they want to portray, and framing the content of their legislation, you may prefer to handpick the students to play leadership roles or to exercise more control over the flow of the simulation. Finally, the timing of the simulation is also flexible. The activities can be spread out over the course of a semester, compressed into a few weeks at the end of a course, or used individually to illustrate or emphasize a particular point. The companion materials provide aids to make this simulation run smoothly for both the students and you, no matter how you decide to integrate it into your classes.

Please feel free to adapt and change assignments, to prioritize assignments differently, and to decide how best to use the particular strengths and weaknesses of the students in your class. Please also make any changes that will improve the flow of the simulation or that will encourage students to participate. In my own courses, I have required some of these activities to be done outside of class time. I have also required students to contact one another outside of class using email and other forms of communication. I have found that students in my courses who participate in this simulation are more often engaged in the class, more likely to do the assigned reading (because they know that it helps them to portray their members and to participate more fully), and report high levels of learning. In making this simulation available to you I hope that you too will experience these positive benefits in your own courses.

Preface

Although I first started doing simulations with students in the fall of 1996, my first experience with a simulation was as a senior in high school. My high school government teacher, Nial Davis, taught us to think about government by "doing" government. He used a simulation called Community Land Use Game (CLUG), which had been developed in the 1960s by Professor Alan Feldt at Columbia University. Even today, almost fifteen years later, I vividly remember role-playing a city council member as we dealt with community development problems, natural disasters, and unscrupulous bankers in our quest to improve our simulated rural town. My experience playing CLUG with my classmates inspired in me a lifelong passion for the study of politics and government.

It was with this experience in mind that, as a teaching assistant for Professor Gary Copeland at the University of Oklahoma during the fall semester of the 1996–1997 academic year, I proposed a simulation of the U.S. Congress. Professor Copeland graciously gave me the freedom to design such a simulation, which I did, and which became the foundation of this simulation.

Many people have assisted me over the years in the development of the simulation. Chief among those are the students that I have the privilege to teach each day. Discussions with my students at the University of Oklahoma, Bucknell University, and Randolph-Macon College have led me to identify new and different techniques that can be used to help students understand the way the Congress works. In particular, Seth Rabinowitz and Jeff Rogan at Bucknell University and Shelley Adolf, Carla Owen, Maria Ciarrocchi, Coleman Adams, Trafton Jordan, Joe Fleury, Curtis Ellis, John Bumgarner, and Ryan Young at Randolph-Macon College have reversed the student/teacher relationship by teaching me new and innovative ways to help others learn.

My husband, John, has also played an especially important role in the development of this project, serving as the guinea pig and sounding board for many of the ideas that ultimately found their way into the project (and for all of the ones that he had the good sense to counsel me to leave out).

Much of the material in this simulation is gathered from participant observation as a member of the 1997–1998 class of the American Political Science Association's Congressional Fellowship Program, which is directed by Jeffrey Biggs. His continuing support has allowed me to continue to be active in pursuing knowledge about the institution of the Congress. Similarly, countless examples of legislative behavior have been supplied by my dear friends Lesli McCollum and Craig Williams, whose jobs on Capitol Hill have given them continuous ringside seats for the show put on daily by the greatest deliberative legislative body in the world.

I owe my colleagues at Bucknell University and Randolph-Macon College a tremendous debt for their support as I sought to integrate innovative teaching methods into my classes on Congress. The faculties in the political science departments at both institutions have been overwhelmingly supportive of new teaching techniques, particularly in the areas of active learning. My current colleagues at Randolph-Macon College, Thomas Badey, Brian Turner, and Bruce Unger, have assisted me immeasurably over the years not just with regard to this simulation, but in terms of helping me to best meet the needs of my students. Moreover, the support of the Dean of the College, Robert Holyer, and my other faculty colleagues has been felt and deeply appreciated.

As every author knows, even single-authored texts are group endeavors. This simulation physically would not exist if not for the dedication of several people involved in its production. David Tatom, Rebecca Green, Reena Thomas, and Janise Fry at Wadsworth have provided countless hours of time, energy, and good counsel in order to improve the quality of this text, while Anne and Greg Draus at Scratchgravel Publishing Services worked wonders with copy editing, layout, design, and production. Finally, I deeply appreciate the comments of the following reviewers who helped me to sharpen my focus and refine this simulation: Michelle Chin, Arizona State University; Scott Meinke, Bucknell University; Daniel Palazzolo, University of Richmond; Ronnee Schreiber, San Diego State University; and Michele Swers, Georgetown University.

1

An Introduction to
the Simulation

One purpose of any course is to immerse students in its subject matter. There is no better way to immerse students of political science in the subject matter of the United States Congress than to have them simulate the experiences of its members and engage themselves in the functioning of the body. For this reason, I developed this simulation of the workings of the United States Congress.

Through this process, you will simulate the U.S. Congress at work. Although the simulation focuses primarily on the House of Representatives, additional optional exercises are included that allow for the class or group to examine the U.S. Senate as well. This simulation focuses on the House for several reasons. First, the House operates under strict rules of procedure and is more easily simulated than the Senate, which operates under more flexible rules. Second, and related, the House vests its leaders with greater institutional power, which allows you, the student, more hands-on control of the simulation itself. Finally, the House membership is far more diverse than the Senate membership—there are far more women and racial and ethnic minorities in the House than there are in the Senate. Thus, although the demographic profile of neither body mirrors the population, the House more accurately reflects the diversity of the American public. This fact provides you with greater opportunities to select members of Congress who mesh well with your own interests, policy preferences, and personal background.

This simulation is meant to be an enjoyable way to assist you in grasping the intricate workings of politics, law, procedure, and legislation in the U.S. Congress. In order for this simulation to work, however, you and your fellow students in the course will have to do your part. Your instructor will act as the Speaker of the House and (if necessary) the presiding officer of the Senate. In his or her capacity as the Speaker or presiding officer, it will be your instructor's job to be focused and organized, to present you with the information you need or with the guidance necessary to find it on your own, and to ensure that the simulation runs smoothly.

Ideally, your instructor will also take precautions to see that the composition of your simulated House of Representatives closely mirrors the demographics, partisanship, geographic distribution, urban/rural distribution, and committee structures of the actual House. In that way, the simulation is structured so that each student has the opportunity to obtain a maximum of hands-on experiences with the legislative process. At the same time, if the simulation is to be effective, *every* student must participate in *every* simulation activity; remember, once the simulation begins, you have a responsibility not only to your simulated Speaker and fellow House members, but to your "constituents," your country, and your conscience as well.

SIMULATION GOALS

You should come to understand several things through your participation in this simulation. They include:

1. The complexity of making legislation
2. The ways in which members of Congress work separately and together to make the laws
3. The role of politics in how Congress works
4. The difficulty members of Congress have in balancing their various commitments to their constituents, their party, their committees, and their own consciences
5. The difficulty of creating new laws
6. The connection between elections and law making

Before describing how the simulation works, it is useful to make note of several important points about the history and evolution of the U.S. Congress. Students, like the members of Congress they will role-play, need to have certain basic information about the Congress in order to fulfill their responsibilities.

THE CONGRESS THEN AND NOW

The U.S. Congress emerged from several important compromises. In 1787, when delegates from the 13 newly independent states gathered in Philadelphia for the Constitutional Convention, the only thing they agreed on was that the Articles of Confederation had not worked. The delegates were divided, however, over whether to create a unicameral (one-chamber) or bicameral (two-chamber) legislative branch. Without debate, but by a vote of seven to three, the delegates opted for a bicameral Congress.[1] They were also divided over the questions of apportionment of seats between large and small states and representation of noncitizens (slaves and Indians). In what has come to be known as the **Great Compromise,** the delegates at the Convention agreed that one chamber, the House of Representatives, would be apportioned based on population, and the other, the Senate, would be equally apportioned with two sena-

Great Compromise Agreement made between large and small states at the Constitutional Convention of 1787 to create a bicameral (two-house) national legislature, with seats in the lower house, the House of Representatives, allocated based on a state's population and seats in the upper house, the United States Senate, allocated equally, two per state.

tors per state. This compromise resolved the tensions between large and small states at the Convention, because it permitted large states a greater number of representatives in the House, but gave the smaller states a representational advantage in the Senate.

In addition to the Great Compromise, the **Three-Fifths Compromise** was also crucial to the creation of the Congress. The delegates agreed that slaves and Indians, although not considered citizens, would be counted as three-fifths of a whole person for the purpose of representation and taxation. This compromise appeased the Southern states—which had previously threatened to leave the Convention—because they would be able to count their slaves toward their total number of representatives in the Congress.

Three-Fifths Compromise
Agreement made between Northern and Southern states at the Constitutional Convention of 1787 to allow slaves and native Americans living within the states to count as three-fifths of a full person for the purposes of taxation and the allocation of seats in the House of Representatives.

The House and Senate were designed to operate differently, in addition to the different apportionment schemes. The House was to be directly elected by the people. Indeed, the House was the only part of the federal government outlined in the Constitution that was to be elected directly and was to be directly accountable to the people. Until passage of the Seventeenth Amendment in 1913, Senators were to be selected by the legislatures of each state. Moreover, the House was given what the framers believed would be a powerful leader, the Speaker of the House, while the Senate would have to be satisfied with a leader who had additional duties as Vice President of the United States.[2] Nonetheless, because of its indirectly elected membership, its advanced age requirement (30 as compared with 25 for House members), and its smaller size, the Senate was intended by the framers to be the wiser, more temperate of the two chambers.

The early Congresses met in New York City or Philadelphia, until a permanent home was found for the national government in Washington, DC, in 1800.[3] Although George Washington had surveyed the area that was to become the national capital, and Washington himself had negotiated the sale of the land to the federal government, by many estimates the new national capital was a disaster. James Sterling Young, in writing about the city of Washington, DC, between 1800 and 1828, points out that President Washington was most likely overcharged for the land that was to become the national capital.[4] As a result, and because Congress had assumed that the capital would pay for itself, initially there was no money appropriated for the construction of government buildings. When construction did begin on the new Capitol building, it was a slow process, and members of the early Congresses lamented the poor state of the Capitol building. In part because of the poor facilities, most members of the early Congresses served only one two-year term, and some did not serve even a full two-year term. Other reasons for the high levels of turnover in the early Congresses include the fact that members of Congress—like the American population more generally—held public service in the fledgling government in low esteem.[5]

Despite the high levels of turnover, the early Congresses were remarkably homogenous. The members of Congress who served during the early part of the nineteenth century were all white and all male. Nearly all of them were farmers and—because of the demanding nature of farm life—found that the part-time nature of the early Congresses suited them just fine.[6] Moreover, most members of the early Congress were wary of appearing power-hungry, so they were reluctant to introduce or champion legislation. As Young points out, the Congress was "out of sight and at a distance" from the people that it represented.[7] For most people, there was little reason to pay attention to the Congress.

Much has changed. Unlike the farmer-legislators of the early nineteenth century, today members of Congress come from all walks of life. Although many are attorneys or have had previous experience working in government at the state or local level, many others come to the Congress from careers in medicine, nursing, or pharmacy (for example, Bill Frist, R-TN; Marion Berry, D-AR; Vic Snyder, D-AR; Eddie Bernice Johnson, D-TX); careers in education (for example, Ed Pastor, D-AZ; Don Young, R-AK; Phil Gramm, R-TX), or careers in business (for example, Tom DeLay, R-TX; Kay Bailey Hutchison, R-TX). A few members still come from careers based in manual labor and agriculture. For example, Senator Ben Nighthorse Campbell, a Republican from Colorado, lists his occupation as "rancher and jewelry designer," and Don Young from Alaska boasts "trapper" as a second career. In short, members of Congress come from varied backgrounds.

What these members have in common, however, is their interest in serving their communities and their fellow citizens and their ability to connect with people. Unlike members of the early Congresses, who were reluctant office-holders, members of Congress today often work diligently to stay in office for several consecutive terms. In some congressional elections, incumbency rates exceed 95 percent. Moreover, where the members of the early Congresses frequently were the only ones willing to stand for election to the office, today a seat in the U.S. Congress is highly coveted by both amateur and professional politicians. This means that each of the 535 men and women who serve in the Congress today have had to be **electable,** possessing a set of important characteristics, including the ability to run a campaign, raise funds, and persuade the public. These skills give constituents confidence in the leadership and policy-making abilities of their member of Congress.

As if running a campaign and winning election were not arduous enough, the transition from "candidate for Congress" to "member of Congress" can also be a difficult one in the modern Congress. Despite a new member orientation session, new members frequently find it difficult to find their way early in their terms. Both the U.S. House and U.S. Senate operate under very specific rules, many of which date back to the First Congress (1789–1790). In addition, each chamber has its own norms—informal, often unwritten, rules—that new members are expected to abide by. In the Senate, these norms include respect for the institution, respect for more senior members, reciprocity, and restrained behavior.[8] New senators are expected to defer to their elder counterparts, and junior senators who seek too much power too soon are punished through institutional mechanisms designed to keep them in their proper place. In the House, the norms include allegiance to political party, respect for the rules of the chamber, and respect for the leadership.

Although new members attend an orientation session to familiarize themselves with the rules, norms, processes, and procedures, most new members lament that there is little that prepares them for the reality of life in Congress. Once in office, members of Congress find themselves attending countless meetings with their party leaders (party caucuses), with their committees (committee hearings, markups, executive business meetings, etc.), with interest groups, and with constituents. As Figure 1 demonstrates, the daily schedule for most members of Congress is often divided into 15-minute increments, sometimes from breakfast through dinner. Not only do members have to attend literally hundreds of meetings per week, but they are also responsible for learning

Electability Possessing a set of characteristics, including the ability to run a campaign, raise money, and persuade the public, that improves a person's chances of being elected to Congress.

Wednesday, March 4, 1998

9:00–9:30 A.M.	Briefing/Work Incentive Bill
9:30–10:00 A.M.	Briefing/Education Roll Out
10:00–10:30 A.M.	Roll Out/Education/S-211
10:30 A.M.	Roll Call Vote Lautenberg Amendment
11:00–11:15 A.M.	Briefing/Jewish Leaders
11:15–11:30 A.M.	Drop-by/Meeting/Jewish Leaders
11:30–12:00 P.M.	Briefing/Secretary Herman
12:15–1:15 P.M.	Lunch/Secretary Herman/Department of Labor
1:15–1:30 P.M.	Briefing/Imported Food Safety/White House—Roosevelt Room
1:30–2:15 P.M.	Press Conference/ImpFoodSafety/White House—Roosevelt Room
2:30–3:00 P.M.	Phone/Office
3:00–3:15 P.M.	Stop-by/Constituent/Office
3:15–3:30 P.M.	Briefing/Senator Gordon Humphrey
3:30–4:00 P.M.	Meeting/Senator Gordon Humphrey
4:00–4:45 P.M.	Briefing/Constituency Inquiry
4:45–5:15 P.M.	Briefing/Naturalization Hearing & Press Conference
5:30–5:45 P.M.	Photo/ U.S. Senate Youth Program
6:00–6:20 P.M.	Meeting/PostmasterGeneral/SR-364

*Modified from a copy of a senator's weekly schedule obtained by the author from a staff member in the senator's office.

FIGURE 1 A Day in the Life of a Member of Congress*

something about the thousands of items of legislation that are introduced each year in the U.S. Congress.

The next chapter addresses the nuts and bolts of the legislative process. It is important to have a solid grasp of the way the legislative process works before proceeding to the simulation itself, which is detailed in Chapter Three. Chapter Three provides instructions for the activities, actions, and processes required to simulate the U.S. Congress. Chapter Four describes resources available for further study of the U.S. Congress. Finally, the appendices provide examples of actual bills and resolutions, examples of **Dear Colleague** letters, and information about how to obtain a job or internship on Capitol Hill.

Dear Colleague letter Letter written from one member of Congress to another to discuss a problem, seek support for a legislative proposal, or announce an event. These letters are an important means of communication and information sharing between members and their staffs.

2

The Legislative Process

Visitors to the Congress from other countries frequently remark that they have no idea how the Congress accomplishes anything. This is because the legislative process used by the Congress is an adaptation of the parliamentary-style legislating that is used in many other parts of the world. But the observations of international visitors about the difficulty of making laws are well founded. In the contemporary Congress, it can take as long as five years for a substantive piece of legislation to wind its way through the time-consuming and complicated legislative process. In addition to the formal steps that legislation must go through, a legislative proposal must overcome a number of informal steps and hurdles before it can become a law. The preceding chapter investigated a bit of the Congress's history. This chapter now turns to providing both an overview and a detailed description of the complex legislative process used by the Congress. It discusses not only the "textbook" steps a proposal must go through but also the other considerations that affect outcomes in the legislative process, such as the role of organized interests, the dynamic nature of the legislative process, and the complexity of legislative decisions.

THE TEXTBOOK LEGISLATIVE PROCESS

The primary purpose of the United States Congress is to make laws, although it also serves other important functions. Indeed, lawmaking is one of Congress's four core functions, and it can be used in the service of at least one of its other functions—representation. (Congress's other functions include oversight of the executive branch and legitimation of the U.S. system of government.) Through the process of making laws, members of Congress engage in a range of activities, including the funding of existing federal government agencies and programs, the creation of new programs and services to serve the needs of the American people, representation of the public's interests, and the staffing of government.

Lawmaking is carried out through the legislative process, a complicated system of information gathering, legislation writing, debate, and voting. Nearly every textbook written for an introductory American government class or course on the U.S. Congress provides a model of the legislative process. It generally depicts or describes the series of steps that a piece of legislation must go through in order to be enacted into law. These steps, outlined in Figure 2, are described throughout the remainder of this chapter.

1. A bill is introduced in the House or in the Senate.

In the House, legislation is dropped into the "hopper," a box on the side of the Speaker's rostrum. In the Senate, senators introduce legislation by reading it from the floor, although Section 2 of Rule XIV of the Senate provides that such reading "may be by title only, unless the Senate in any case shall otherwise order."[1] Members can introduce several different types of legislation. Most legislation gets the title of "**bill.**" In order for a bill to become a law, both the House and the Senate must pass it in identical form and the president must approve it. Bills can take one of two forms. The first is a **public bill.** Public bills are items of legislation that affect the general welfare or address a general question. In contrast, **private bills** are pieces of legislation that focus on individual matters that affect a specific person (for example, a bill granting diplomatic immunity to a prominent foreign leader). Bills are numbered in the order in which they are introduced in the Congress, with the exception of any numbers that have been reserved by the leadership for "special" legislation or leadership priorities. **Joint resolutions** are essentially the same as bills, in that they must be approved in identical form and signed by the president if they are to take effect. However, joint resolutions are typically reserved for matters of limited scope (for example, an emergency appropriation of funds); they are frequently used to authorize military action and for proposed constitutional amendments.[2] Joint resolutions are identified by the designation "H.J. Res." in the House of Representatives.

In contrast to a bill or a joint resolution, a **simple resolution** is used when the item of legislation is relevant only to the house of Congress in which it was introduced. This type of legislation is not presented to the other chamber for consideration, nor is it presented to the president for signature. Examples of resolutions include legislation that expresses the sense of one house or the other on a matter of public controversy and legislation that commends or censures a member of a chamber for his or her behavior. Resolutions receive the designation "H.Res."

Concurrent resolutions are similar to joint resolutions, in that they must be passed in identical form by both houses of Congress. However, unlike bills and joint resolutions, concurrent resolutions are not sent to the president for signature (in this sense, concurrent resolutions are similar to simple resolutions). Also, unlike bills and joint resolutions, concurrent resolutions—even when passed by both houses—do not have the force of law. Instead, these are used to express a sense of both houses of Congress, or to make a policy change that affects only the Congress, such as fixing a time for adjournment or creating joint committees within the Congress. Concurrent resolutions receive the designation "H.Con. Res." when they are introduced in the House.

bill A piece of legislation; requires approval in identical form by both houses of the Congress and must be signed by the president in order to have the effect of law.

public bill A bill that addresses a general question or whose passage affects the general welfare of the United States.

private bill A bill that focuses on a specific individual or on a matter that affects a specific individual.

joint resolution Another type of legislation; like a bill, must be passed in identical form by both houses of Congress and approved by the president. Unlike public bills, joint resolutions are typically used for matters of limited scope.

simple resolution Used when an item of pending business affects only one house of Congress; needs the approval of only a single house of Congress in order to take effect, and is binding only on the house of Congress that passes it.

concurrent resolution Another type of legislation, similar to a joint resolution, that must be passed by both houses of Congress. However, it is not sent to the president for signature and does not have the force of law, even when passed in identical form. Concurrent resolutions are used to make policy changes that affects only the Congress.

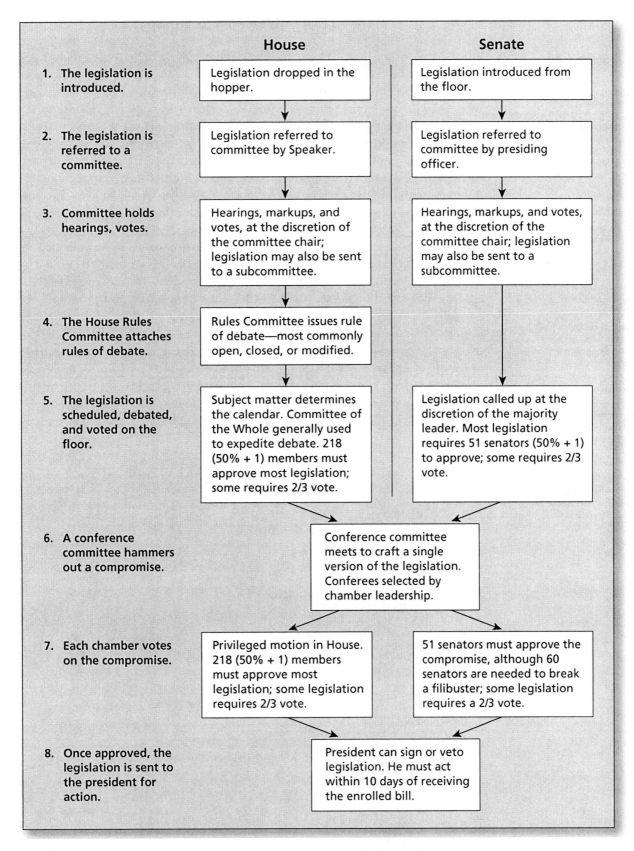

FIGURE 2 The Legislative Process

2. The legislation is referred to a committee.

Once a bill or resolution has been introduced, it must be sent to a committee in the Congress to be processed. There are three main types of committees in Congress: **standing committees,** which are established to be permanent and with fixed jurisdictions; **select** or **special committees,** which are temporary committees set up to deal with a specific problem; and **joint committees,** which are committees—either standing or special—that include members of Congress from both chambers. In the House, legislation is almost always sent to at least one standing committee; the Speaker of the House ultimately determines the committee to which a bill or resolution will be referred. In the Senate, the presiding officer of the Senate makes the referral. In both chambers, however, the parliamentarians are integrally involved with decisions about bill referrals because a bill must be referred to the **committee of jurisdiction**—the standing committee that has jurisdiction over the subject matter of the legislation, as determined by the rules of the two chambers. In some cases, a piece of legislation can be referred to more than one committee. In the House, the Speaker of the House has discretion to refer the bill to more than one committee (a so-called **multiple referral**); in the Senate, multiple referrals are possible only by a majority vote of the chamber upon the request of the majority or minority leader.[3]

Currently, the House has 19 standing committees, as called for in the Standing Rules of the U.S. House of Representatives. They are:

Committee on Agriculture

Committee on Appropriations

Committee on Armed Services

Committee on the Budget

Committee on Education and the Workforce

Committee on Energy and Commerce

Committee on Financial Services

Committee on Government Reform

Committee on House Administration

Committee on International Relations

Committee on the Judiciary

Committee on Resources

Committee on Rules

Committee on Science

Committee on Small Business

Committee on Standards of Official Conduct

Committee on Transportation and Infrastructure

Committee on Veterans Affairs

Committee on Ways and Means

The Senate currently has 16 standing committees. They are:

Committee on Agriculture, Nutrition, and Forestry

Committee on Appropriations

Committee on Armed Services

Committee on Banking, Housing, and Urban Affairs

standing committee A committee of either the House of Representatives or the U.S. Senate whose jurisdiction is fixed according to the rules of the chamber. These committees are permanent, in that they cannot be eliminated nor their jurisdiction changed without altering the standing rules of the chamber.

select (special) committee A committee, sometimes temporary, with limited jurisdiction. Select committees rarely consider legislative proposals but may provide policy guidance or conduct investigations.

joint committee A congressional committee made up of members of both the House and the Senate.

committee of jurisdiction The standing committee in the House or the Senate that has the responsibility, per the standing rules of the chamber, to hear a particular piece of legislation based upon its subject matter.

multiple referral The referral of a piece of legislation by the Speaker of the House or presiding officer of the Senate to more than one committee for processing.

Committee on Budget

Committee on Commerce, Science, and Transportation

Committee on Energy and Natural Resources

Committee on Environment and Public Works

Committee on Finance

Committee on Foreign Relations

Committee on Governmental Affairs

Committee on Health, Education, Labor, and Pensions

Committee on Judiciary

Committee on Rules and Administration

Committee on Small Business and Entrepreneurship

Committee on Veterans Affairs

Each of the standing committees in the House and Senate sets its own rules (which can be reviewed by visiting the committees' Web sites at www.house.gov or www.senate.gov). Common to all committees, however, is that the chair of the committee has an extraordinary amount of control over the committee's agenda.

In addition to the standing committees of the House and Senate, there are a number of select and joint committees. Although these committees rarely consider legislative proposals, they may be used to provide guidance on policy initiatives or to gather information related to public policy making. They are:

House Permanent Select Committee on Intelligence

House Select Committee on Homeland Security★

Joint Committee on Printing

Joint Committee on Taxation

Joint Economic Committee

Senate Select Committee on Ethics

Senate Select Committee on Indian Affairs

Senate Select Committee on Intelligence

Senate Special Committee on Aging

Proposed legislation does not have to go to the same committee in the House that it goes to in the Senate. As is clear from the lists above, in some cases there are not equivalent committees in each chamber. Therefore, all legislative proposals are sent to the committee that is most appropriate in the House and the committee that is most appropriate in the Senate.

3. The committee(s) of jurisdiction hold(s) hearings on the bill, debate(s) it, and then sometimes pass(es) it out of committee and back to the full House or Senate.

The committee or committees of jurisdiction usually do the work of preparing a bill or resolution to be debated by the full chamber. As Professors Christopher Deering and Steven Smith write in *Committees in Congress,* "In the modern

---

★This committee will become a permanent standing committee in the House of Representatives.

Congress, committees have three primary powers: collecting information through hearings and investigations, drafting the actual language of bills and resolutions, and reporting legislation to their parent chambers for consideration."[4] Every committee in the Congress is empowered to hold hearings on any proposals that are referred to it. These committees also have the power to subpoena witnesses and documents that are deemed crucial to the full understanding of a legislative proposal. With the exception of the House and Senate Intelligence and Appropriations Committees, the hearings held by congressional committees are open to the public.

markup Step in committee processing of legislation in which the members of the committee amend the pending legislation.

Once hearings are held, the committee will hold a **markup** on the legislation. This is the time when members of the committee are able to amend the legislation to make it more acceptable to them. During the markup, the members of the committee meet in the committee room to discuss their proposed amendments. It is a time to add to, strike from, or alter the existing language of the legislation. Depending upon the subject matter and length of the legislation, the markup process can take a few hours or a few weeks.

Following the markup, the committee will schedule the bill or resolution for a vote. These votes take place during the committee's regularly scheduled executive business meeting. When it is time to vote, members of the committee who support the legislation will speak on its behalf and the members who oppose it will speak against it. Then the committee clerk will call the roll, and members will announce their decisions on the proposal. A majority of members of the committee must vote in favor of the legislation in order for it to be sent to the floor. If there is a tie vote in committee, the bill or resolution is almost always dead. In rare cases, legislation will be sent to the full chamber even though it did not get a majority to support it in committee. These rare instances generally include such important legislative business as Supreme Court nominees in the Senate, or major leadership priorities in both chambers.

4. In the House, a bill passed by a standing committee is sent to the Rules Committee, where a rule of debate is attached.

Once legislation has been passed by the relevant committee(s) of jurisdiction in the House, it is sent to the House Rules Committee, whose job it is to attach a rule of debate. The House Rules Committee serves to promote the interest of the majority party leadership. The majority party dominates the Rules Committee with a supermajority of nine majority party members compared to only four minority party members. As a result, it is very difficult for the minority party to assert its will; to draft a rule for a bill that favors the minority party, the four minority party members would need to convince three majority party members of the committee to agree. Thus, it is with good reason that the House Rules Committee is sometimes called the Speaker's Committee, because its efforts have a disproportionately beneficial impact on the majority party and it is the Speaker who makes the appointments to the committee.

Open rule A rule of debate in the House of Representatives that permits any member of the House to offer any germane amendment to the pending legislation.

The Rules Committee can attach a number of rules; among the more common are open rules, closed rules, and modified rules. **Open rules** permit any members to offer any germane amendments to the legislation when it is brought up for debate. **Closed rules,** on the other hand, prohibit any amendments at all from being made to the legislation, although these rules often permit a substitute to be offered to the entire proposal. **Modified rules** permit some amendments. Modified open rules allow more amendments than do modified closed rules, which typically permit only a handful of amendments, or amendments to only a part of the legislation. As described in a 1981 House Rules Committee Report, modified rules "usually limit the amendments to a pending measure to those offered by the committee with jurisdiction over the bill, or provide that only specified amendments may be considered, or provide that amendments may be offered to certain titles or sections of the measure and not to others."[5] In recent years, the House Rules Committee has been less willing to grant open rules for legislation than it once was. As Davidson and Oleszek point out, in the 95th Congress (1977–79), 85 percent of rules issued by the House Rules Committee were open rules; in the 106th Congress (1999–2001), only 51 percent of rules issued by the Committee were open.[6]

Once the Rules Committee has approved a rule of debate, the rule must be approved by the full House in order for the legislation to be considered. If the rule fails in the House, the legislation to which it was attached is considered to be dead as well. This is because there is no mechanism to determine how debate on the measure will proceed in the absence of a rule. However, as Oleszek explains:

> The House seldom rejects a rule proposed by the Rules Committee. . . . The Rules Committee generally understands the conditions the House will accept for debating and amending important bills. Further, it is an expectation within the majority party that support for rules is a given and that deviations from this behavioral norm could be held against a lawmaker when, for example, plum committee assignments are handed out.[7]

5. The bill is scheduled on the House or Senate floor, where it is then debated and voted on before being sent to the other chamber for approval.

Once a rule has been attached to a piece of pending legislation, that legislation is eligible to be scheduled for floor debate. Although scheduling legislation seems as though it ought to be a simple process, in reality scheduling legislation can be quite complicated. For example, the House has five different calendars. The **union calendar** is reserved for bills that deal with revenues and expenditures, including taxation and appropriations bills. The **house calendar** is reserved for nonmoney bills of major importance; most substantive measures will be placed on this calendar. The **corrections calendar** is used for noncontroversial measures that address "laws and regulations that are ambiguous, arbitrary, or ludicrous."[8] Measures on this calendar can only be brought up on certain days of the month—generally, the second and fourth Tuesdays, at the discretion of the Speaker of the House.[9] The **private calendar** is used to schedule private bills, discussed above. Like the corrections calendar, this calendar is only in order on certain days of the month—generally the first and third Tuesdays of the month, although this is also at the Speaker's discretion.[10] Finally, the **discharge calendar** is used to schedule legislation that has been forced out of committee through a **discharge petition.**[11]

Closed rule A rule of debate in the House of Representatives that prohibits nearly all amendments from being made to the pending legislation.

Modified rule A rule of debate in the House of Representatives that permits some amendments to pending legislation, but usually limits the members who are able to offer amendments.

union calendar A calendar used by the House of Representatives that is reserved for bills that deal with revenues and expenditures, including taxation and appropriations bills.

house calendar A calendar used by the House of Representatives that is reserved for nonmoney bills of major importance. Most substantive measures are placed on this calendar.

corrections calendar A calendar used by the House of Representatives for noncontroversial measures. Measures on this calendar can only be brought up on certain days of the month, at the Speaker's discretion.

private calendar A calendar used by the House of Representatives to schedule private bills. Like the corrections calendar, the private calendar is only in order on certain days of the month, at the Speaker's discretion.

discharge calendar A calendar used by the House of Representatives to schedule legislation that has been forced out of committee through a discharge petition.

discharge petition A petition of 218 members of the House of Representatives that forces a piece of legislation out of committee over the objection of the committee's members or the committee chair. This is often used to circumvent committee chairs' prerogative to determine whether or not to move a piece of legislation to a committee vote.

Once legislation has been placed on one of these House calendars, it can be called up for consideration at the discretion of the Speaker of the House. The Speaker is not obligated to call up the legislation in the order in which it was placed on the calendar; in fact, policy and political considerations are far more likely to determine the order by which the House considers legislation.

The House adds another complication to the debate and passage of legislation: the Committee of the Whole House on the State of the Union. The **Committee of the Whole,** as it is called, is a procedural device designed to enhance the legislative process in the House. The Committee of the Whole, like the House of Representatives itself, meets in the House chamber, but it uses procedures designed to expedite the amendment process. Indeed, most legislation is actually debated in the Committee of the Whole, which requires a quorum of 100 (as compared with the House of Representatives, which requires a quorum of 218). There are also very strict time constraints imposed in the Committee of the Whole, limiting the amount of time for the offering of amendments. Meeting as the Committee of the Whole permits the House to make significantly more progress on pending legislation than it could possibly make if it used the rules of the House to structure debate, because the debate rules used by the full House can be manipulated much more easily to prevent the passage of legislation.

Once the work of amending the legislation is done, the Committee of the Whole reports the amended measure back to the House of Representatives, which must then vote to accept the amendments. This process is sometimes confusing to outsiders, because the very same members who voted to approve the amendments in the Committee of the Whole vote again to approve them in the House of Representatives. One surefire way to tell whether the members are meeting in the Committee of the Whole or in the House of Representatives is to look at the mace, a tall staff that sits near the Speaker's right hand. When the mace is up, the members are meeting as the House of Representatives. When the mace is down, the members are meeting in the Committee of the Whole.

In contrast to the complex and formal legislative procedure of the House, the Senate uses less complicated and less structured rules of procedure. Instead of the varied calendars of the House, the Senate has only two calendars. Nearly all the legislative business of the Senate is scheduled on the **legislative calendar,** with the exception of treaties and presidential nominations, which are placed on the **executive calendar.** Unlike the House, the Senate switches easily between calendars at the discretion of the **majority leader.** In the Senate, legislation can be brought to the floor either through a **unanimous consent request,** which is a request to the chamber from the majority leader to consider a piece of legislation, or through a **unanimous consent agreement,** which is an agreement between the **majority leader** and the **minority leader** to consider legislation. Unanimous consent requests are used primarily for noncontroversial legislation. Since the objection of a single member can prevent the legislation from being brought up, unanimous consent requests are used only when the majority leader is certain that he or she has the support of the membership of the Senate to proceed to consideration of a bill or resolution.

When the majority leader is unsure whether or not he or she can count on the support of other senators, it is more likely that a unanimous consent agreement will be worked out. These agreements are made between the majority

Committee of the Whole Short for Committee of the Whole House on the State of the Union, the Committee of the Whole is used for floor debate in the House of Representatives. There are significant procedural advantages to meeting as the Committee of the Whole, including expedited rules of debate and relaxed requirements for a quorum.

legislative calendar One of two calendars used by the United States Senate. This calendar is used for scheduling legislative proposals.

executive calendar The second of two calendars used by the United States Senate. This calendar is used for scheduling executive branch items that require the Senate's approval, such as nominations to the executive and judicial branches, and treaties.

unanimous consent request In the context of scheduling legislation, a request from the majority leader to the rest of the senators in the chamber to consider a piece of legislation. In other contexts, a unanimous consent request is a request made by any member of the Senate to his or her fellow senators asking that all senators agree to whatever the senator has proposed to do.

unanimous consent agreement An agreement negotiated between the Senate majority and minority leaders agreeing to bring up an item of pending business and agreeing to specific terms of debate. These agreements, at least theoretically, indicate that no member of the Senate from either party will object to the terms of debate agreed to by the leadership.

majority leader Floor leader of the majority party in both the House and the Senate. This individual is responsible for managing floor debate for the majority party.

minority leader Floor leader of the minority party in both the House and the Senate. This individual manages floor debate for the minority party.

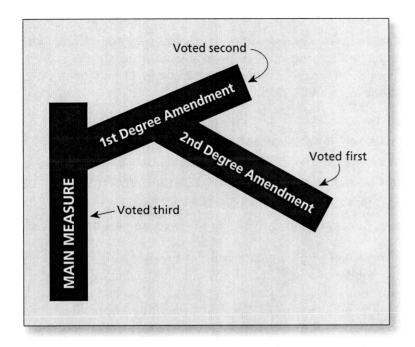

FIGURE 3 Amendment Tree

leader, the minority leader, committee chairs, and any senators with an interest in the pending legislation.[12] The purpose of these agreements is to avoid obstruction and delay from obstinate senators. These obstructionist tactics can take the form of **holds**—requests to the majority leader not to bring legislation or nominations to the floor for a vote—or **filibusters.** Unanimous consent agreements also specify the time and date that debate on a measure will begin.

Once legislation has been scheduled in the chamber, it will be brought to the floor under the procedures specified by the Rules Committee (in the House) or by the unanimous consent agreement (in the Senate). During floor debate in the House, only germane amendments—those related to the subject matter of the legislation—are permitted, and are debated subject to the rule attached by the Rules Committee. The Senate does not have a germaneness requirement, which means that any amendment that a senator wishes to offer will be in order. In both the House and the Senate, the amending process is governed by the **amendment tree,** so called because when drawn, it looks like a tree trunk with many protruding branches. The amendment tree specifies the nature of amendments and the order in which they will be voted upon.

Although the amendment tree shown in Figure 3 is oversimplified, it illustrates the major principles of voting on amendments to legislation. Second-degree amendments are the first amendments to be voted on, because they affect the content of the first-degree amendments. Once the second-degree amendments have been disposed of, the first-degree amendments are acted upon. It is also important to note that there are two kinds of first-degree amendments: perfecting and substitute amendments. **Substitute amendments** strike one or more sections of a piece of legislation and replace them wholesale with new language. **Perfecting amendments** seek to adapt the existing language of a section or sections to be more acceptable to members of the House or the Senate.

hold A request from a senator to the majority leader not to bring a piece of pending legislation to the floor for a vote.

filibuster A procedural delaying tactic most commonly invoked in the United States Senate, where once a member has the floor, he or she can hold it until such time as 60 senators vote to end debate. This allows a single senator, or a small group of senators, to block action on pending business with which they disagree.

amendment tree A visual representation of the order of voting on proposed amendments to an item of pending legislative business.

substitute amendment An amendment that strikes a section or sections of pending legislation and replaces what was stricken with entirely new language.

perfecting amendment An amendment that adapts, but does not take the place of, the existing language of the proposed measure.

In both the House and the Senate, most legislation requires only a majority vote to be approved. There are a few exceptions to this rule, however. For example, rules changes and new taxation proposals require a supermajority vote in the Senate. Once the bill or resolution is passed by one chamber, the other chamber must pass it in identical form.

6. If the two chambers pass different versions, the bill will almost always go to a conference committee made up of members from both the House and the Senate. When that happens, that committee will hammer out a compromise, and both chambers will vote on the compromise version.

conference committee A temporary, joint committee made up of members of both the House and the Senate. The purpose of these committees is to resolve differences in legislation passed by both the House and the Senate. The conference committee is typically the last step before final passage of a piece of legislation in the U.S. Congress.

Conference committees are temporary committees consisting of members of both the House and the Senate. When the House and the Senate pass different versions of the same legislative proposal, members of both chambers will meet to work out the differences. The Speaker of the House formally selects House conferees; Senate conferees are formally selected by the majority leader. In both chambers, the conferees generally come from the standing committee that had jurisdiction over the legislation and that originally considered the proposal. Conference committees usually consist of anywhere from 5 to 20 members, although there have been conference committees with well over 100 members sitting as conferees. For example, Sinclair notes that the conference committee for a 1988 trade bill had 199 conferees.[13]

The conferees from each chamber roughly represent the partisan breakdown of membership in the chamber.[14] In conference, each chamber gets one vote; typically, the conferees from each chamber will attempt to reach a consensus on how to cast that vote. In some cases, the conferees will take a vote among themselves to determine how to cast their single vote. According to political scientist Ross Baker, the Senate appears to prevail more frequently than the House on contested conference votes.[15]

Conference committees wield a tremendous amount of power. They have the ability to dramatically alter legislation; there have even been instances when conference committees have stricken all but the enacting clause of legislation and inserted the text of a separate proposal that the conferees preferred. The reason that conference committees are so powerful is that their work product—the final conference report that refers the legislation back to each chamber for a final vote—is sent back to both chambers as a **privileged motion,** meaning the legislation can no longer be amended. Once this privileged bill is back on the House or Senate floor, it is rare that either chamber will vote to reject it, because by that time it is a completed piece of legislation. Neither chamber can amend the legislation, nor can either chamber vote to reject it; if either of those events happens, the legislation is dead.

privileged motion A motion that must be addressed ahead of all other pending motions.

7. Once the bill passes each chamber in identical form, it is sent to the president for approval.

enrolled bill Legislation passed in identical form by both the House of Representatives and the United States Senate.

Once a bill or resolution passes both chambers in identical form, the **enrolled bill** is sent to the president, who has ten days to decide whether to sign it into law, veto it, or do nothing. If the president signs it, the text becomes law according to the provisions of the legislation. To veto the legislation, the president pens a veto message and returns the legislation to the Secretary of the House and Secretary of the Senate. If the president does nothing, the legislation either dies or becomes law without signature, depending on whether Congress adjourns during the ten days set aside for the president to act. If the Congress remains in session and the president fails to act, the proposal will become law without signature. If Congress adjourns before the president has acted, the measure is dead. This latter circumstance is known as a **pocket veto.**

pocket veto Once both houses of Congress pass a piece of legislation in identical form, the president has ten days to sign it into law or veto it. If Congress adjourns during that ten-day period and the president has not acted, the measure does not become law.

WHAT THE TEXTBOOKS
UNDEREMPHASIZE

Although the information provided by the textbook model of the legislative process is not incorrect, it neglects many of the political realities of the contemporary Congress, such as the large congressional staff, logrolling and legislative cue taking, and the high levels of partisanship. All of these traits have characterized the contemporary legislative process in recent decades.

Today, congressional staffs dominate the legislative process off the House and Senate floors. In fact, staff members outnumber elected members of Congress by a ratio of 57 to 1.[16] Staff members are integrally involved in members' office operations, where they answer phone calls, meet with constituents and lobbyists, and engage in constituency service projects. Indeed, nearly all constituency service is handled by staff members rather than members of Congress themselves. Congressional staffs are also important actors in the lawmaking process. Staff members research legislation, draft legislation and amendments, and are even responsible for determining legislators' strategies. Staff attend committee hearings and markups, and may be called upon to be active in these processes when members of Congress have questions about a legislative proposal. In short, there is virtually no aspect of the legislative process that is not affected by congressional staff members.

However, members' staffs appear to be a more important part of the legislative process in the Senate than in the House. This is because the Senate has larger staffs and Senate staff members tend to have more years of experience than their House counterparts. An example of the role of staff in the Senate comes from political scientist Ross Baker, who quotes former Senator Richard Schweiker's description of a meeting of five senators. The senators were cosponsors of a piece of legislation and were meeting to work out their differences. According to Schweiker, "We went to this senator's office who called the meeting and he didn't do any of the talking. . . . He delegated to his staff the entire job of working this thing out and he sat there and had his staff be the prominent players with four of his colleagues. It was an insult. . . . A lot of times I've seen that happen in the Senate."[17] Staff members also frequently accompany their bosses to the House or Senate floor to provide support or expertise.

In addition to an increased role for congressional staff, logrolling (vote trading) and **legislative cue taking** appear to be increasing. Members of Congress are called upon to discuss, debate, and vote on thousands of legislative proposals in any given two-year Congress. There is no way that members can possibly review each of these proposals in a comprehensive or thorough way. Moreover, as one sitting senator points out, some members of the Senate do not always do

legislative cue taking The practice of members of Congress seeking advice from like-minded interest groups and fellow members about how to vote on a piece of legislation.

their homework on a proposal. So, "when it comes time to vote, they find someone on the committee and ask him how to vote."[18] As a result, members rely not only on their staffs but also on other members of Congress for information about legislation and for cues about how to vote. This makes sense in the time-constrained environment of the House and Senate; by consulting with a member of the committee of jurisdiction, the members can save themselves valuable time and effort. Sometimes, members agree to trade their vote with other members in exchange for others' support on the legislative priorities that they care about.

This raises another important aspect of the legislative process that has been neglected by many textbooks: the processes through which legislators make decisions about pending proposals. Most of the influences on legislators—including staff members, interest groups, the president, and professional policy researchers—are treated as separate from decision making. Indeed, a few previous studies have even suggested that members' legislative decisions are made free from the influence of their staffs. These studies neglect the reality that interest groups, staff members, and policy experts frequently drive members' decision making, especially on issues that members of Congress know or care little about.

Lastly, partisanship has increased in the Congress in recent years. Although partisanship has always been important in the House because that chamber's rules are organized to promote the interests of the majority party, partisanship has been increasing in both the House and the Senate. According to Professor Ross Baker, "Relations between the parties . . . became worse after the 1994 Republican takeover."[19] Democrats, borrowing from the Republicans' playbook, began to delay legislation and increased their levels of partisan rhetoric. This was even more apparent in the Senate, where norms of respect and reciprocity had always allowed members from both parties to work together. Beginning in the 1980s, however, party politics became more important in the Senate. Between 1981 and 1986, when Republicans controlled both the Senate and White House, it was very important to the Republican party to have loyalty from its members. When Democrats regained control in 1987, they responded to the Republicans by challenging President Reagan frequently, setting up even greater partisan conflicts. The Republicans ratcheted up their partisan attacks when they assumed the majority in 1995. This was due in part to an influx of new senators who had previously been members of the House, where partisanship is demanded. It was also due to the personalities of Senate leaders like Tom Daschle and Trent Lott, who did not work well together during the late 1990s. During both the 1980s and 1990s, the use of—or threat to use—the filibuster in the Senate increased dramatically over the levels of use in the 1970s, despite changes to Senate rules that made it easier to end a filibuster.[20]

Other, less obvious changes to the legislative process have taken place in recent years as well. For example, congressional scholar Barbara Sinclair, in *Unorthodox Lawmaking: New Legislative Processes in the U.S. Congress,* notes an increase in the use of special rules of debate and complicated parliamentary maneuvers in the legislative process.[21] Another change that Sinclair points out is an increase in the use of **omnibus legislation**—"legislation that addresses numerous and not necessarily related subjects, issues, and programs, and therefore is usually highly complex and long."[22] Political scientist Glen Krutz notes that members of Congress have increased their use of omnibus legislation because it has proven to be an efficient way of getting around partisan gridlock.

omnibus legislation Complicated and lengthy legislative proposals that address substantial numbers of public policy questions in a single measure.

Controversial provisions are frequently accepted without question because of the need to pass the major provisions of the omnibus bills. Omnibus legislation is appealing to members because it can provide them with political cover; rather than explaining their vote on a controversial provision, they can focus on the noncontroversial or more significant aspects of the legislation to divert attention from the parts of the legislation about which their constituents are unhappy.[22]

The next chapter describes the simulation. As you prepare to simulate the workings of the U.S. Congress, you should refer back to this section as necessary to remind you of the ways that the processes you are simulating are carried out by the actual U.S. Congress.

3

The Simulation

Congratulations on your election to the United States Congress! Now that you've been elected, you have new challenges to face. Not only do you have to meet the daily demands of reviewing legislative proposals and working with other members of Congress, you must be accountable to your constituents as well. Constituents generally demand that their representatives do something for them, and members of Congress will, if they want to be reelected. "Doing something" generally includes such legislative activities as procuring resources, goods, or services for the district, providing essential services, and assisting constituents with understanding federal programs. The activities in this simulation also assume that each of you, at some point in the simulation, will fit Mayhew's description of members of Congress as "single-minded seekers of reelection,"[1] because unless you are reelected, you will not be able to pursue your other policy goals. The bottom line is that each participant in the simulation is expected to do something.

As a member of Congress, you will draft one bill, a bill justification, and a "Dear Colleague" letter. In addition, you will be expected to contribute to any and all committee meetings held during class time, and to be present and play a part in floor debate and final passage of all legislation. In addition, participants may be called upon to testify as a witness during the hearings held by the congressional committees, or by any other committees, throughout the semester. Remember that passage of your bill by the committee of jurisdiction and by the full House may depend wholly on your ability to persuade your colleagues. Finally, you'll be called upon to explain yourselves to your constituents. As Professor Richard Fenno explains in *Home Style: House Members in Their Districts*, members of Congress spend much of their time back in their districts explaining their legislative voting decisions to their constituents. You will do this through a constituency newsletter.

This simulation is intended to be an enjoyable but thought-provoking way to learn about the legislative process. Your instructor will act as the Speaker of the House, and it will be his or her job to monitor your progress and help you acquire the resources you need to perform your duties as a member of Congress. In that sense, your instructor will from time to time fulfill roles that, in the real Congress, would be carried out by staff. (Of course, some of the things you'll be doing—such as actually drafting legislation—are also done by staff in the real Congress.)

Your instructor will also set the specific policies and procedures related to the evaluation, grading, and weighting of the simulation assignments. In some cases, your instructor may opt to change or omit procedures that are specified in this chapter in order to make the simulation run smoothly. For that reason, you'll need to pay particular attention to the Speaker—just as the members of the actual United States House of Representatives must pay attention to the Speaker if they want to be certain to accomplish their goals.

Of course, before getting started, you'll first need to decide who you are! To get you thinking about what sort of member of Congress you want to be, the next section describes the membership of the current Congress. At the end of the section, it will be time for you to make some decisions about whom you would like to portray.

WHO ARE THE MEMBERS OF
THE CURRENT CONGRESS?

As noted in the introduction to the simulation, members of Congress (also known as MCs) come from varied and diverse backgrounds. There is no one path to the U.S. Congress, although there are several common ways that members get to Capitol Hill—frequently through careers in business or the law.

Recently, congressional scholars have explored the question "Who runs for Congress?" Most congressional scholars agree that the people who choose to run are ambitious, believe that they can win the election, and are good fundraisers. Congressional candidates also consider the national climate in making their decisions to run. As two congressional scholars note:

> Politicians do act strategically. Their career decisions are influenced by their assessment of a variable political environment. Their choices reflect, among other things, the conventional wisdom that national events and conditions affect individual voting behavior. National phenomena thought to be important are consistently monitored and noted; indicators abound. More and better candidates appear when signs are favorable, worse and fewer when they are unfavorable.[2]

In the conclusion to his edited volume *Who Runs for Congress*, Thomas Kazee notes that, in general, those individuals who decide to run for a seat in Congress are "serious politicians," for whom "politics is at the center of their lives."[3] He adds that those who run for Congress—who, ultimately, become members of Congress—are frequently ambitious entrepreneurs who run because they believe they can win, and who often put personal and career interests on hold in order to seek elective office.[4] They frequently want to stay in the Congress for a reasonably lengthy period of time and will mold their constituency styles and congressional career in order to continue to be elected.[5] In short, many of today's members of Congress are highly political people. At the very least, many of them are "second-career" politicians, a term I use to mean those members of Congress who, having worked for a while in a particular career, leave that career to devote their remaining working years to public service as a member of Congress.

Today's congressional membership remains dominated by men who come from careers in fields like law and business, although the Congress is less dominated by this archetypal member than it was ten or twenty years ago. Although the Congress is a long way from representing descriptively the diverse age, race, gender, economic, and labor background of the U.S. population as a whole, it is more descriptively representative now than it was a decade ago.

The 2003 Congressional Research Service report "Membership of the 108th Congress: A Profile" notes that in the most recent Congress there were

~76 female members (62 in the House, 14 in the Senate)

~25 Hispanic members of the House of Representatives

~39 African American members of the House of Representatives

~7 Asian/Pacific Islanders (2 in the Senate; 5 in the House).[6]

The average length of service for members of the House was nine years, and the average tenure for senators was approximately eleven years.[7] The average age of members across both houses was 53.9; Representative Adam Putnam (R–FL) was the youngest member of Congress at 28, and Representative Benjamin Gilman (R–NY) was the oldest at 78.[8]

Both the current (108th) and immediate past Congress include a former first lady of the United States (Hillary Rodham Clinton), as well as several former governors, two additional former state first ladies, 275 former state legislators, 111 former congressional staff members, and several doctors.[9] A significant number of members also come from the business and legal professions.[10] In addition, the CRS Report notes that several members of Congress come from interesting and diverse backgrounds, noting that the occupations of the members of the 108th Congress include:

an astronaut, a professional magician, a semi-professional musician, two broadcasters, a television sportscaster, a television reporter, a motivational speaker, a commercial airlines pilot, a corporate pilot, a flight school instructor, a major league baseball player, a major league football player (who was also a college football coach), a florist, a librarian, two vintners;

and

two auctioneers, two jewelry makers, a steelworker, a carpenter, an iron-worker, a paper mill worker, a river boat captain, a hotel bellhop, a taxicab driver, a race track blacksmith, and a "jackeroo" (cowboy) on a sheep–cattle ranch. [11]

The diverse backgrounds of members should not be surprising in light of the incredibly diverse backgrounds of the American people.

SIMULATION ASSIGNMENT 1:
SELECTING A MEMBER OF CONGRESS

Your first assignment as a member of the simulated Congress is to determine which member of Congress you would like to play. When you think about what kind of member you would feel comfortable portraying, you may wish to consider such factors as party affiliation, gender, and home state. However, you may not want to choose someone who is just like you or with whom you identify. For example, although portraying a member of Congress who shares your party affiliation might create less internal tension within you, portraying a member of Congress who is not a member of the same political party as you are will give you the experience of exploring the issue positions and motivations of the other party, which in turn may give you greater insights into your own choice of party affiliation. Similarly, although it may be more comfortable to portray a member of Congress who is the same gender as you, selecting a female member of Congress if you are a man, or a male member of Congress if you are a woman, might provide a unique perspective on the representational issues related to gender that confront women and men in the Congress. Finally, although selecting a member from your home district or home state can be fun, because that member's constituents are your friends and neighbors, selecting a member from somewhere else can help you broaden your understanding of the issues confronting other parts of the country.

The Member Selection Sheet, which is on the next, tear-out page, will ask you to select at least three members of Congress that you would be willing to play during the simulation from a list of fifty or so current members of the 108th Congress. It also asks you whether you want to be a member of the leadership in the simulated House of Representatives. During the first party caucus, each party will have the responsibility of selecting its leaders and committee chairs from a list of willing students. Members of the Republican party will select a majority leader, majority **whip,** and committee chairs for each of the five committees. Members of the Democratic party will select a minority leader, minority whip, and committee **ranking members** for each of the five committees.

whip This person works for either the majority or the minority party. It is his or her job to ensure party discipline and keep track of members' commitments to vote on a piece of legislation. On party priorities, it is the whip's job to ensure sufficient votes to pass or kill the bill or resolution.

ranking member The highest-ranking member of the minority party serving on a committee.

The job of the majority and minority leaders in this simulation, just as in the actual House of Representatives, is to represent their respective parties to the Speaker and before the full House of Representatives. The committee chair will be responsible for maintaining a clear agenda for the committee, including a schedule for hearings and markups. In addition, the chair will be responsible for contacting authors of legislation to inform them of the date/time their legislation will be discussed by the committee and to call them to testify on its behalf, should the committee so desire. The job of the ranking member—the highest-ranking member of the minority party on the committee—is to work with the chair to determine which legislation will be considered, to represent his or her party's interests, and to assist the chair with carrying out any of his or her aforementioned duties. For the most part, the performance of these leadership positions should require only minimal amounts of additional work or time.

Please be sure that you fill out the Member Selection Sheet carefully and completely. This will help your instructor to assign you and your classmates to members of Congress in a way that maximizes the geographic diversity of the membership, as well as tries to approximate the actual race, gender, age, and partisan composition of the House.

MEMBER SELECTION SHEET

Your Name _____

I   *DO*   *DO NOT*   (circle one)   want to be a member of the leadership.

Please rank your top three preferences for a member of Congress to portray during the simulation from the list of members of the 108th Congress, below. For more information about these members and to help guide your choice, visit their Web sites, which are accessible at http://www.house.gov. Their committee assignments in the simulated House appear underneath their names. Please note that while every effort will be made to assign you to one of your top three choices, there is no guarantee. Your instructor reserves the right to alter committee assignments and/or member selections in order to ensure partisan, gender, geographic, racial/ethnic, and committee diversity.

_____ Robert "Bud" Cramer (D-AL)
Economic Affairs

_____ Don Young (R-AK)
Infrastructure

_____ John Shadegg (R-AZ)
Economic Affairs

_____ Vic Snyder (D-AR)
IR/NS

_____ Lynn Woolsey (D-CA)
Health, Education and Welfare

_____ Tom Lantos (D-CA)
IR/NS

_____ George Radanovich (R-CA)
Government

_____ Xavier Becerra (D-CA)
Economic Affairs

_____ Mary Bono (R-CA)
Government

_____ Diana DeGette (D-CO)
Economic Affairs

_____ Christopher Shays (R-CT)
Economic Affairs

_____ Michael Castle (R-DE)
Health, Education, and Welfare

_____ John Mica (R-FL)
Government

_____ Alcee Hastings (D-FL)
IR/NS

_____ Bennie Thompson (D-MS)
IR/NS

_____ Neil Abercrombie (D-HI)
Infrastructure

_____ Ann Northup (R-KY)
Infrastructure

_____ Henry Hyde (R-IL)
Government

_____ Jerry Weller (R-IL)
Economic Affairs

_____ Dan Burton (R-IN)
IR/NS

_____ Jim Leach (R-IA)
Economic Affairs

_____ Kenny Holshof (R-MO)
Health, Education, and Welfare

_____ Charles Stenholm (D-TX)
Infrastructure

_____ Sheila Jackson Lee (D-TX)
Government

_____ Lamar Smith (R-TX)
Government

_____ Jim Ryun (R-KS)
Economic Affairs

_____ Edward Whitfield (R-KY)
Infrastructure

_____ W. J. "Billy" Tauzin (R-LA)
Infrastructure

_____ John Baldacci (D-ME)
Infrastructure

_____ Steny Hoyer (D-MD)
Economic Affairs

_____ Barney Frank (D-MA)
Government

_____ John Conyers (D-MI)
Government

_____ Jim Ramstad (R-MN)
Economic Affairs

_____ Charles "Chip" Pickering Jr.
(R-MS) Infrastructure

_____ Charles Taylor (R-NC)
IR/NS

_____ Doug Bereuter (R-NE)
Infrastructure

_____ Shelley Berkley (D-NV)
Infrastructure

_____ Jennifer Dunn (R-WA)
Health, Education, and Welfare

(continued)

MEMBER SELECTION SHEET (*continued*)

_____ Carolyn McCarthy (D-NY)
Government

_____ Vito Fossella (R-NY)
Economic Affairs

_____ Zoe Lofgren (D-CA)
Infrastructure

_____ Sherrod Brown (D-OH)
Health, Education, Welfare

_____ Chaka Fattah (D-PA)
Economic Affairs

_____ Bud Shuster (R-PA)
Infrastructure

_____ Robert Goodlatte (R-VA)
Health, Education, and Welfare

_____ Patrick Kennedy (D-RI)
Infrastructure

_____ Bart Gordon (D-TN)
Infrastructure

_____ Bernard Sanders (I-VT)
Economic Affairs

_____ Bob Goodlatte (R-VA)
Government

_____ James Moran (D-VA)
Economic Affairs

_____ Thomas Petri (R-WI)
Health, Education, Welfare

_____ Barbara Cubin (R-WY)
Infrastructure

_____ Tom DeLay (R-TX)
Economic Affairs

_____ Ray LaHood (R-IL)
IR/NS

_____ Anna Eshoo (D-CA)
IR/NS

_____ Vernon Ehlers (R-MI)
Health, Education, and Welfare

_____ Jay Inslee (D-WA)
IR/NS

_____ Henry Bonilla (R-TX)
Government

_____ Martin Meehan (D-MA)
Economic Affairs

_____ Mike Ferguson (R-NJ)
Health, Education, and Welfare

_____ Mike Simpson (R-ID)
Infrastructure

_____ Ernest Istook (R-OK)
Government

_____ Brad Carson (D-OK)
Health, Education, and Welfare

_____ Ruben Hinojosa (D-TX)
Government

_____ Sanford Bishop (D-GA)
Economic Affairs

_____ Steve Buyer (R-IN)
Government

_____ Judy Biggert (R-IL)
Health, Education, and Welfare

_____ Charles Bass (R-NH)
IR/NS

_____ Tom Allen (D-ME)
Infrastructure

_____ George Nethercutt (R-WA)
IR/NS

_____ Darlene Hooley (D-OR)
Economic Affairs

_____ Marcy Kaptur (D-OH)
IR/NS

_____ Jeff Flake (R-AZ)
Government

_____ John Sweeney (R-NY)
Infrastructure

_____ Bob Etheridge (D-NC)
Health, Education, and Welfare

_____ Steve Chabot (R-OH)
Government

_____ Denny Rehberg (R-MT)
Infrastructure

WHERE CAN I FIND INFORMATION
ABOUT MEMBERS OF CONGRESS?

As you are thinking about which member you want to play, or once you have been assigned to play a particular member of Congress in the simulation, it will be essential to seek out information about members of Congress. Information about members of Congress is available from a number of sources. Some of them are more informative and appropriate than others. Some potentially useful sources are listed below:

- The U.S. Congress online at http://www.house.gov and http://www. senate.gov. These are the official Web sites of the U.S. Congress. From here, you can access the official Web sites of each member of the House and Senate by following the links to the members' individual sites.

- http://thomas.loc.gov. This is the Congress's online information site. It provides links to substantial amounts of information about members' voting records, their sponsorship of bills and resolutions, and their committee and floor votes, as well as links to additional Internet and textual sources of information about members, their legislation, and the legislative process more generally.

- Michael Barone, Richard E. Cohen, and Charles E. Cook, Jr., *The Almanac of American Politics* (Washington, DC: National Journal Group, 2004). A comprehensive biographical guide to members of Congress and their districts. Some information is available at www.nationaljournal.com.

- *Congress at Your Fingertips* (Washington, DC: Capitol Advantage, 2003). A handheld quick guide to the members, staff, and committees in the Congress.

- Brian Nutting and H. Amy Stern, eds., *Politics in America* (Washington, DC: Congressional Quarterly Press, 2004). A comprehensive biographical guide to members of Congress and their districts.

- Norman Ornstein, Thomas Mann, and Michael Malbin, *Vital Statistics on Congress, 2001–2002* (Washington, DC: Congressional Quarterly Press, 2002). A series of statistics covering everything from members of Congress to legislative outputs to staffing levels.

- J. Michael Sharp, *Directory of Congressional Voting Scores and Interest Group Ratings*, 2d ed. (Washington, DC: Congressional Quarterly Press, 1997). A comprehensive guide to the voting and ideological scores that prominent interest groups use to rate members of Congress. Organized alphabetically by the member's name.

- Project Vote Smart: A nonpartisan, nonprofit organization dedicated to improving the public's familiarity with candidates for public office, Project Vote Smart maintains a comprehensive Web site—www.vote-smart.org— that makes available data collected from candidate surveys.

SIMULATION ASSIGNMENT 2:
MEMBER PROFILE

By this point in the simulation, each of you will have been assigned to play the role of a member of the United States House of Representatives. In order to play the part as thoroughly and as accurately as possible, your first assignment is to draft a profile of your member of Congress. The profile should be written as if the member him/herself actually did the writing (so, it should be written in the first person: "I am a member of Congress from the second district…," etc.). Your profile should include the following information:

- The member's personal background (age, race, gender, religion, education, occupation, legislative style, etc.)
- The location, size, and population demographics of the member's congressional district
- The main industry or enterprise within the member's district, if any
- The member's primary concerns and issue positions
- The length of time the member has been in Congress
- The electoral circumstances of the last election (won with large majority, won with small majority, beat an incumbent, etc.)
- Any additional information that provides insight into your member of Congress

A worksheet has been included on the following page to assist you with compiling your profile. Keep in mind that the more detail you provide in your profile, the better able you will be to play the role you are assigned. You should use the major sources of information about the Congress, including *The Almanac of American Politics* and *Politics in America*. Both of these are available in the reference section of most college and university libraries. You may also wish to visit the House of Representatives' Web site at http://www.house.gov.

MEMBER PROFILE WORKSHEET

Your name _____

Your member's name_____

Member's state_____ Member's district_____

Population of member's district_____

Demographic Profile of the District

_____ Men (percent)   _____ Women (percent)

_____ African American (percent)   _____ Asian (percent)

_____ Hispanic (percent)   _____ White (percent)

_____ College-educated (percent)

Major corporations, industries, or enterprises

_____   _____

_____   _____

_____   _____

Distinguishing natural or geographic features of the district

_____   _____

_____   _____

Other distinguishing or interesting features of the district

_____   _____

_____   _____

Demographic Characteristics of Member

Member's party affiliation_____

Career prior to entering the Congress_____

Number of years of service in Congress_____

Highest level of education attained_____

Married? _____ Yes   _____ No

_____ Number of years

Children? _____Yes   _____ No

_____Number of children

Member's Most Recent Election

Percent of the vote won _____

Opponent(s') name(s)

_____   _____

_____   _____

(continued)

MEMBER PROFILE WORKSHEET (*continued*)

Major campaign themes or promises

_____   _____

_____   _____

Major campaign contributors, including dollar amounts (see www.fec.gov or www.opensecrets.org for this information)

_____   _____

_____   _____

_____   _____

Member's Policy Priorities

Member's current or previous committee assignments

_____   _____

_____   _____

_____   _____

Member's policy priorities

_____   _____

_____   _____

_____   _____

Sources of Information About Member Used in This Assignment

1. _____

2. _____

3. _____

HOW MEMBERS ORGANIZE THEMSELVES

One defining feature of the U.S. Congress is the fragmented nature of the institution. Its organizational structure is such that members find themselves reporting to multiple "masters." For example, the political parties in the Congress determine the leadership of the chambers, who chairs committees, who sits on the committees, and what the chamber's legislative priorities should be. However, committee chairs have nearly complete autonomy to determine which legislative proposals their committees will hear and act upon. Thus, among the organizational structures that members must confront as they attempt to represent the best interests of their constituents, and the best interest of the country, are party caucuses and committees, each of which will be discussed below.

PARTY CAUCUSES

Especially in the House, but in the Senate as well, the political parties are alive and thriving. In fact, the parties represent the most overarching organizational structure in both chambers. The **party caucuses** are important for a number of reasons. First, they provide an opportunity for members to meet alone with their fellow partisans to discuss legislative priorities and legislative strategy. They also provide a forum for the selection of chamber and committee leadership and for the selection of committee members. The leaders of the party caucuses are considered to be the fourth-highest ranking members of the House and Senate leadership. The Web site of the House Democratic Caucus describes its role as follows:

party caucus/conference
Organization composed of the members of the chamber from a specific party; used to discuss legislative priorities and legislative strategy, as well as to select members of the leadership and of committees. Each party has its own caucus or conference in each chamber.

> The Democratic Caucus is a service-oriented organization for all Democratic Members of the U.S. House of Representatives. As the only subgroup within the House of which every Democrat is a Member, the Caucus seeks to achieve consensus and to ensure Members have the tools to implement it. The Caucus nominates and elects the House Democratic Leadership, approves committee assignments, makes Caucus rules, enforces party discipline, and serves as a forum to develop and communicate party policy and legislative priorities. It accomplishes these tasks through weekly Caucus Meetings, on-going Issue Task Forces, the yearly Caucus Issues Conference, periodic special events, and continual Member-to-Member communication.[12]

Although the House Republican Party does not provide a similar description on its Web site, its caucus performs the same functions for House Republicans as the House Democratic Caucus does for House Democrats.

The Senate caucuses are both similar to and different from the House caucuses. The Senate caucuses (or **conferences,** as they are called in that chamber) are similar in that they are responsible for choosing leaders, selecting committee members, and dealing with the general organizational structure of the chamber and the party. However, the Senate conferences differ from their House counterparts in that each Senate Conference also has a separate Policy Committee, whose job it is to discuss policy priorities and positions for the party. This means that the caucuses themselves are service providers for the senators who belong to them, rather than forums for debate and discussion. For example, the Senate Republican Conference Web site notes: "Over the last century, the mission of the Conference has expanded and been shaped as a means of informing the media of the opinions and activities of Senate Republicans. Today the Senate Republican Conference assists Republican Senators by providing a full range of communications services including Graphics, Radio, Television, and Internet."[13]

SIMULATION EXERCISE: PARTY CAUCUSES

The first simulation activity, once you have been assigned to portray a member of Congress, is for each political party to assemble its members in a party caucus. Just as in the real House of Representatives, party caucuses are an opportunity for each party to choose its leadership, including the majority and minority leaders as well as committee chairs and ranking members. During the first party caucus, each party will have the responsibility of selecting its leaders and committee chairs. No member may serve in more than one leadership position, and *each of these leadership positions must be filled in order to proceed with the simulation*. Therefore, your instructor will reserve the right to assign students to play these roles if there are not sufficient volunteers.

In addition to choosing leaders, the parties will likely want to discuss what they view as their party-specific priorities. These priorities should be acceptable to most members of the caucus, and should reflect the issues that the members of the *simulation* caucus care about. (Please note that these priorities may or may not reflect the priorities of the actual Republican and Democratic parties, although they will probably not be vastly different.) The caucuses may also want to establish a plan for "opposition research"—that is, for determining whether certain members of the other party are likely to be helpful or harmful to the party's goals.

It is not necessary at this stage for the party to determine which legislation it wants to see passed, or what the party's legislative strategy will be. A second party caucus, following the conclusion of committee action on all legislation, will be used for those purposes. That second caucus is described later in this chapter.

WRITING LEGISLATION

Legislative Counsel's Office
The nonpartisan legislative drafting service used by members of Congress and their staffs.

In this section, we turn to the very important task of drafting legislation. Legislation is the vehicle through which changes to public policy are made. Every member of Congress is actively engaged in sponsoring legislation, in large part because members are generally sincere in wanting to create good public policy, which often requires the passage of legislation. Enacting legislation is also a tangible way to demonstrate to constituents that you, as a member, are respected and that you have accomplished something. However, most members of Congress receive substantial amounts of assistance with drafting legislation. This assistance comes in the form of staff help from their personal staffs, their committee staffs, and ultimately, the House and Senate Legislative Counsels' Offices. The **Legislative Counsel's Office** is "the legislative drafting service."[14]

The Office of Legislative Counsel for the House of Representatives consists of 35 staff attorneys, whose job it is to provide "drafting and related assistance to the Members of the House, the House committees, and the conference committees between the House and the Senate."[15] These attorneys are impartial, and their work with members of the House is subject to attorney–client privilege, meaning that their communication with members and their staffs is confidential.

SIMULATION ASSIGNMENT 3:
WRITING LEGISLATION

Unfortunately, you do not have a legislative counsel's office at your disposal. Therefore, the drafting of legislation will be exclusively your responsibility. (Keep in mind that some members and staffs do write their own legislation, so this is not entirely out of the realm of real-life circumstances.) To that end, the following guide may be helpful to you. There is also a worksheet at the back of this section that will help you to organize your thoughts.

Step 1: Determine the type of legislation
that you are proposing.

Remember that in the House of Representatives, there are four major types of legislation: bills, resolutions, joint resolutions, and concurrent resolutions. Each of these was described earlier, but recall that most legislation gets the title "bill," and that there are two kinds of bills—public and private. A resolution is used when the item of legislation is relevant only to the house of the Congress in which it was introduced. Joint resolutions are essentially the same as bills, in that they must be approved in identical form and signed by the president if they are to take effect. Finally, concurrent resolutions are used to express a sense of both houses of Congress, or to make a policy change that affects only the Congress, such as fixing a time for adjournment or creating joint committees within the Congress. Once you have determined the type of legislation you are drafting, you will want to indicate it on your legislation, leaving a blank space for the number, as shown on the legislation worksheet at the end of this section of the simulation. For the purpose of the simulation, the Speaker will assign each piece of legislation a number, just as legislation is assigned a number in the actual House.

Step 2: Determine on which calendar your
legislation should be scheduled.

As if it isn't complicated enough that the House has four different types of legislation (the Senate does too, for that matter), you will recall that the House also has five different calendars. To remind you, these are as follows:

- *Union Calendar.* This calendar is reserved for money bills (that is, bills that deal with revenues and expenditures, including appropriations bills).

- *House Calendar.* This calendar is reserved for nonmoney bills of major importance. Most substantive measures will be placed on this calendar.
- *Corrections Calendar.* This calendar is used for noncontroversial measures.
- *Private Calendar.* This calendar is used to schedule private bills, discussed above.
- *Discharge Calendar.* This calendar is used to schedule legislation that has been forced out of committee by a discharge petition. (It is unlikely—although not impossible—that your bill will be scheduled on this calendar. At the time you are drafting your legislation, you should assume that your legislation will be sent to one of the other calendars.)

Step 3. Write the bill.

Now that you have determined the type of legislation you're writing and the appropriate calendar for your legislation, the next step is to figure out what you want it to say.

Step 3a. Write a statement of purpose for the legislation you intend to propose. Some elements are common to all pieces of legislation. For example, every piece of legislation has a statement of purpose that can be found directly beneath its number. This statement of purpose explains what the bill is about. If you look at the sample legislation in Appendix I, you'll notice that these statements of purpose come immediately following the notation "A bill (or joint resolution, etc.) to . . . ," as shown on the Legislation Worksheet.

Step 3b. Make a note on your worksheet as to which type of enacting or resolving clause is appropriate. In most legislation, following the statement of purpose (which you will notice appears twice on your worksheet) is an **enacting clause** or a **resolving clause.** Enacting clauses are appropriate for bills; a resolving clause is appropriate for all types of resolutions. Without these clauses, legislation has no effect. So, every piece of legislation includes the appropriate enacting or resolving clause.

enacting/resolving clauses
The clauses at the beginning of pieces of legislation that require the provisions of the legislation to take effect upon its passage by the Congress and, when appropriate, after it is signed by the president.

Step 3c. Give your legislation a title. In addition to a statement of purpose, most major legislation also includes a title—that is, a way of referring to the legislation. Sometimes these titles are simply descriptive ("Nuclear Threat Reduction Act"); other times, they can be catchy phrases or even can be converted to easy-to-remember acronyms (Racketeer Influenced and Corrupt Organizations Act becomes RICO). It is said on Capitol Hill that one thing to be careful of is what acronym your title might create. For obvious reasons, an environmentally friendly member of Congress wouldn't want to introduce anti-dumping legislation with the title "A Ban Against Dumping In Deteriorating Environmental Areas Act"—no one would vote for A BAD IDEA Act. Where it says "Short Title" on your worksheet, fill in the title of your legislation.

Components of the Legislation

Once you have finished with the preliminaries, it is time to get serious about drafting your legislation. You can find some examples of actual pieces of legisla-

See p. 75

[handwritten margin note: Bill must be at least 2.5 pages]

tion in Appendix I to help guide your thinking about the format; additional examples of bills and resolutions are available at http://thomas.loc.gov.

Step 3d. Draft at least one, but as many as are needed, statements of findings or "whereas" clauses for your legislation. Many pieces of legislation include some justification for the legislation. In the case of bills, this justification, when it is included, usually takes the form of a **statement of findings;** it usually comes in the second section of the bill, just after the title. In resolutions, these findings are often presented as "whereas" clauses (see the concurrent resolution in Appendix I for an example). Either way, you will need to present some justification for your legislation.

statement of findings The justification, often included in bills and resolutions, for why the legislative proposal is necessary.

Step 3e. Outline the major themes of your legislation. The remainder of the legislation should be focused on the substance of what it is you are trying to accomplish. If you are writing a resolution, you will "resolve" to do what it is you want to do. If you are writing a bill, you will simply declare what it is you are doing.

As you write the remainder of the legislation, you will need to separate your main ideas into major headings and include details about each as subheadings, or subsections, as shown on the worksheet. Attach additional sheets as necessary. These details could include the appropriation of funds to support the legislation; they might specify to whom the legislation will apply (the whole country? specific states? specific people?); and/or these details may simply clarify your major themes. It may be easiest for you to think about the rest of the legislation as an outline. You should again refer to the sample pieces of legislation in Appendix I to help guide you through this process.

Step 3f. Draft the appropriate sunrise and sunset provisions for your legislation. The last major components of your legislation are appropriate "sunrise" and "sunset" provisions. A **sunrise provision** sets a date for the legislation to take effect. A **sunset provision** sets a date—if you so desire—for the legislation to expire. All legislation includes some form of sunrise provision indicating when it will take effect. Some legislation—especially pilot programs, and certain types of regulations—includes a sunset provision.

sunrise provision The date on which an item of legislation will take effect.

sunset provision The date on which a law will expire.

LEGISLATION WORKSHEET

(Circle calendar type)   *Union   House   Corrections   Private*   Calendar

107th CONGRESS
2nd Session

(Circle legislation type)   H.R.   H.J.Res.   H. Con. Res.   H. Res. _____
(Leave blank for bill number.)

A Bill/Resolution (circle appropriate type) to

_____ *(Explain the purpose of your legislation here.)*

IN THE HOUSE OF REPRESENTATIVES

_____

<u>YOUR MEMBER'S NAME HERE</u> introduced the following bill, which was referred to the
Committee on _____ *(Leave a blank; the Speaker will fill in the Committee of Referral.)*

A BILL/RESOLUTION (circle appropriate type)

To _____
   (Explain the purpose of your legislation again here; it should be identical to the purpose you stated above.)

Be it enacted by the Senate and House of Representatives of the United States of
America in Congress assembled, (*This is the enactment clause; you must include this
if you are drafting a bill.*)

OR

Resolved by the House of Representatives of the United States of America in
Congress assembled, (*You must include this resolving clause in all resolutions; add
the Senate [as above] if it is a joint or concurrent resolution.*)

SECTION 1. SHORT TITLE

This Act may be cited as _____
(Give your legislation a title here.)

(continued)

LEGISLATION WORKSHEET (*continued***)**

SECTION 2. FINDINGS OR WHEREAS CLAUSES
(*In this section, you should give a justification for why this legislation is necessary.*)

A. _____
_____
_____
_____

B. _____
_____
_____
_____

SECTION 3: (*Indicate here what your legislation is doing. You can use as many subsections as are needed.*)

A. _____
_____
_____
_____

B. _____
_____
_____
_____

C. _____
_____
_____
_____

SECTION 4: Date of Enactment (*Here is where any sunrise clause should be placed.*)

_____
_____
_____
_____

SECTION 5: (optional) Expiration Date (*Here is where any sunset clause should be placed.*)

_____
_____
_____
_____

Some Tips for Bill Writing

Here are some general guidelines to keep in mind as you draft your legislation.

- Be as specific as possible.
- Be certain you have addressed potential conflicts and concerns that other members might have.
- Be sure to indicate whether any money should be appropriated and, if so, how much.
- Be sure to indicate how the legislation will be administered. Will it be self-executing, need the states for implementation, or be implemented by federal bureaucratic processes (which ones)?
- Be certain that your legislation reflects your member's goals and priorities, both for the district and for the country.

SIMULATION ASSIGNMENT 4: DEAR COLLEAGUE LETTER

Once a member of Congress drafts legislation, he or she knows that it will be a long, hard road to passage. In each two-year Congress, thousands of bills and resolutions are introduced. Although the total number of pieces of legislation has declined from the all-time high of more than 26,000 during the 90th and 91st Congresses, the 106th Congress (1999–2000) considered 10,280 pieces of legislation.[16]

In light of the large number of pieces of legislation, members of Congress use a number of persuasive techniques to convince their colleagues that their legislation ought to be passed. This is not easy; roughly 5 percent of all legislation introduced is actually passed by the Congress.

Passing legislation can be especially difficult because a member of Congress cannot always count on the full support of his or her political party. In order to reach beyond party lines and raise the interest of as many of their fellow members as possible, many members of Congress use "Dear Colleague" letters to introduce their legislation to their colleagues, to highlight the need for their legislation, and to set their legislation apart from the (literally) thousands of other pending bills and resolutions.

The format of the Dear Colleague letter is simple. It is almost always a one-page letter from a member of Congress written to fellow members. It introduces the member's proposal, offers some rationale for it, and encourages his or her colleagues to cast a vote in favor. Early on in the legislative process, Dear Colleague letters are frequently used to generate cosponsors for a legislative proposal. Securing both a large number of cosponsors and powerful cosponsors—such as members of the leadership or prominent committee chairs—can be important in setting a legislative proposal apart from the thousands that are introduced in each Congress.

Sometimes multiple cosponsors will sign Dear Colleague letters. (For this initial assignment, you don't have that luxury, although you are welcome to write additional Dear Colleague letters once you have added cosponsors to your legislation.) Two examples of Dear Colleague letters are provided in Appendix II to give you an indication of the appropriate format for such letters.

SIMULATION ASSIGNMENT 5:
BILL JUSTIFICATION

At least 2 pages

In addition to your Dear Colleague letter, it is important for the integrity of the simulation that you spend some time considering why it is that you are proposing your legislation. That is, you need to determine what values you are trying to maximize, what benefits and costs will be incurred by your constituents, and whether you have written a bill that is legitimately within the realm of concern of the member of Congress you have been assigned to portray. For that reason, the next assignment requires that you draft a relatively brief reflective essay about your project, using the guidelines that follow.

Assume that you are writing a letter to a constituent who wants to know why you introduced the legislation you introduced. As any member of Congress would, you should respond to this constituent with a thoughtful explanation of why the bill is important. This response should address different themes from the Dear Colleague letter, although some of the information and/or explanation may overlap. In justifying your legislation, you will likely want to explain to the constituent:

- Why you, as the specific member of Congress that you are portraying, think that this legislation is important

- How this legislation is in keeping with your stated legislative goals and priorities

- How this legislation is consistent with your past activities in the House—or if it is inconsistent, why you believe this inconsistency is rational and justified

- How this legislation will benefit your constituents—or if it is not directly related to your constituents, why you have chosen to introduce legislation that is more national in scope

It is important to think through all of these issues to be certain that you are accurately portraying your member, and to make it easier for you to ensure that you have a foundation on which to base your arguments in support of your legislation. In other words, this assignment works to ensure that you are being conscious of your member's priorities, not your own, throughout the simulation.

SIMULATION ASSIGNMENT 6:
ADDING COSPONSORS

cosponsors Additional members of Congress who are willing to put their names on a piece of legislation authored by another member or members.

Once you have drafted your legislation, you will want to seek out **cosponsors**—other members of Congress who share your perspective and are willing to put their names on your legislation. In order to do that, you will want to do some research on the voting records of your fellow members to determine whether any of them have previously supported legislation similar to the bill or resolution you have proposed. In addition, you may wish to consider with which interest groups other members have relationships. Interest groups are often involved in the cosponsorship process because they put pressure on members to support particular pieces of legislation. If you believe that one or more of your colleagues should be willing to cosponsor your legislation, you should seek them out and ask them to sign on to your bill. On the next page are two cosponsor forms that you can tear out and use for this purpose.

Cosponsorship generally—although not always—means that you can count on the support of your cosponsor when it comes to debating the legislation in committee or on the floor. It also means that you have leverage over the party leadership, because the more sponsors your bill has, the easier it will be for the leadership to move the legislation once it's on the floor (since there would be fewer people in a position to obstruct the flow of debate on it). Keep in mind that not all legislation has more than one sponsor; some legislation is so particular or specific, or so controversial, that other members are hesitant about supporting it. Thus, although you will certainly want to try your hardest to find cosponsors, you may not be successful—and that's okay.

As you consider whether to cosponsor other members' legislation, you may wish to ask yourself the following questions:

- How will this piece of legislation affect my constituents?
- How will this piece of legislation affect the country as a whole?
- How do I (as the member of Congress) personally feel about this?
- How do my fellow party members feel about this legislation?
- Could this legislation be amended to improve it?
- Could this legislation be amended to provide a good or service to my constituents, if one is not already provided?
- How will I explain my vote for or against this legislation?

COSPONSOR FORM

Member Name_____

Legislation Title_____

By signing my name to this form, I agree to cosponsor the legislation named above.

Student Name	Member Name	Signature

- -

COSPONSOR FORM

Member Name_____

Legislation Title_____

By signing my name to this form, I agree to cosponsor the legislation named above.

Student Name	Member Name	Signature

COMMITTEES

Once the caucuses have met to establish the leadership of the simulated House and the individual members of Congress have drafted their legislation, the five committees of the simulation will take control of the legislation assigned to them by the Speaker. Remember that the committees used in this simulation are aggregations of the committees that actually exist in the House of Representatives. (This is necessary because trying to run the simulation with 19 committees would not be feasible.)

The committees in the simulation, just like the committees in the House of Representatives, are charged with the task of preparing legislative proposals for floor debate. Committees have been called the "workhorses" or the "workshops" of the Congress[17] because so much of the work of members of Congress is done in these committees. Each committee operates differently from every other committee. Some are extremely partisan; in others, members tend to work together across party lines. Some committees, such as the Health, Education, Labor, and Pensions Committee in the House, are constituency-focused; others, such as the Foreign Relations Committee in the Senate, rarely consider constituency-based legislation.

As noted in the previous chapter, in the current Congress, the Senate has 16 standing full committees and 68 subcommittees. The full committee with the largest number of subcommittees is Appropriations, which alone has 13 subcommittees (one for each of the major appropriations bills) under its jurisdiction. Several Senate committees, including Ethics, Indian Affairs, Veterans' Affairs, and Small Business and Entrepreneurship, have no subcommittees. The House of Representatives has 19 full standing committees, with a total of 88 subcommittees.[18] It is at the discretion of the committee chair whether to send items of pending business to a subcommittee or to hold the legislation at the full committee. However, proposed constitutional amendments are nearly always referred to a subcommittee for additional scrutiny. If a subcommittee first considers the legislation, the full committee must still approve it before it can be scheduled on the floor.

SIMULATION EXERCISE:
COMMITTEE MEETINGS

Once bills have been turned in, the Speaker will assign each bill to the appropriate committee of jurisdiction. The simulated House will have five committees (remember, in reality the House of Representatives has 19 standing committees, as well as several joint committees and numerous subcommittees). Your bill will be assigned to the committee that has jurisdiction over its subject matter. Multiple referrals are possible. The Speaker (your instructor) will make the determination as to which committee is most appropriate based on the following descriptions of the committees.

Infrastructure The Committee on Infrastructure will consider all legislation that deals specifically with transportation, national resources, and science and technology issues. These issues include, but are not limited to, agriculture, forestry, ecology, energy policy, environmental policy, emerging technologies, highways and public roads, bridges, railways, airline regulation, and air travel.

International Relations/National Security The IR/NS Committee will consider all legislation dealing with bilateral or multilateral relationships between the United States and other countries. It will also consider any legislation dealing with international trade, global markets, espionage, diplomacy, drug trafficking and interdiction, the military, base closures, and immigration.

Health, Education, and Welfare The Health, Education, and Welfare Committee will consider all legislation that deals with health, education, and welfare issues. These issues include, but are not limited to, health care policy, Medicare, Medicaid, pharmaceutical drugs, Social Security, Aid to Families with Dependent Children (and other poverty programs), education policy, teacher testing, national testing standards, and student loans.

Economic Affairs The economic affairs committee will review any piece of legislation that deals with interstate trade, labor issues, consumer protection and consumer affairs, securities and exchange (the stock market, antitrust, monopolies, etc.), work-incentive programs, or other economic issues. This committee will also take on the responsibility of the House Ways and Means Committee, and will be responsible for reviewing legislation referred to it to determine its effects on the U.S. budget. Such legislation would include anything proposing a tax increase or tax cut.

Government and Judiciary The Government and Judiciary Committee will deal with all internal matters relating to the workings or the conduct of government, reforms of the House or other government entities, and rules for members of the legislative branch. Issues such as crime, drugs, abortion, and gun control would also fall under this committee's jurisdiction. In addition, this committee will deal with any veterans' issues.

Notes on Committee Work

Keep in mind that it may not be possible for every committee to debate and vote on every piece of legislation during the time set aside in class. In reality, the committees in the House of Representatives and the Senate do not hear, debate, and vote on every proposal brought to them during any given Congress. This is because of the volume of legislation and the time-consuming nature of committee work, and because the committee chair has discretion whether or not to hear a piece of legislation; when the chair opposes a legislative proposal, it is unusual for it to be given the committee's attention. *It will be at the chair's discretion, in consultation with the ranking member, to determine which legislation to consider or not consider.* So, the committees in the simulation should not necessarily feel obligated to hear every piece of legislation referred to them. They must, however, use the time set aside for committee meetings productively. Remember that when the committees consider legislation, they generally are sincere in their desire to make improvements to allow the legislation a fair chance on the House or Senate floor. Therefore, committee members in the simulation should also take care to ensure that they are considering legislation fairly and with an eye toward making it acceptable to members of Congress from both parties.

Once the committee decides to hear your legislation, the committee chair will schedule it for a hearing. As a member of a committee, or when you testify before a committee that is considering your legislation, you should expect to build support for your legislation; this is the first step toward seeing that your bill has a chance of being voted out of committee. (You may wish to convince colleagues to cosponsor your legislation. Two cosponsor forms are included at the end of the previous section. Cosponsor forms may be turned in after legislation has been referred to committee, and at any point up until the full House session.) Sometimes you may be called before a committee other than the one you sit on to testify on behalf of your legislation. You will simply need to leave your committee meeting and attend the other committee's hearing. Remember, if you fail to testify on behalf of your own legislation, it is far less likely to survive committee consideration intact.

Once the committee has completed its hearings, it will then proceed to a markup session. A markup is similar to the idea of a revision—the committee will literally mark up your legislation with suggested changes to language or content. Members with an interest in the legislation will frequently present amendments to add language to, or delete a passage from, the legislation. During the markup, both substantive language changes and minor technical corrections are made.

Your committee should follow the same model for the markup. You should be prepared to offer amendments to legislation that is troubling to you. In particular, you should seek to amend legislation to provide benefits and services for your constituents, to make the legislation more acceptable to your party, and to ensure that the final product that comes out of committee has a reasonable chance of passage on the floor. Once the bill has been marked up, the committee will take a vote on its passage. If a majority of the committee members support the legislation, it is considered to have been voted out of committee and will be eligible to be scheduled on the floor.

Once a bill is voted out of committee, the bill's author must be informed by the committee chair of any changes made during the markup. It will then be the responsibility of the author to draft a final version of the bill that reflects the committee's changes, and to submit that revised bill to the Speaker with sufficient time for copies to be made and distributed prior to the full House session. The revised legislation must be accurate; the committee chair and ranking member, who will be responsible for managing debate on the legislation that comes out of their committee, will act as a check on the bill's author.

A day or two before the start of floor debate (or before the convening of the Rules Committee, should the Speaker opt to use one), the Speaker will provide each member of the House with copies—either paper or electronic—of all legislation that is to be debated. It is the responsibility of all members of the House to have read all legislation and to be prepared to debate each item of pending business on the floor.

The House Rules Committee

In the House of Representatives, as noted in the previous chapter, all legislation that is approved by a committee with jurisdiction over substantive legislative proposals must also be given a rule of debate by the House Rules

Committee. These rules determine what sections of the legislation can be amended during floor debate. The House Rules Committee also allows the majority party to control debate, because the committee has a supermajority of members of the majority party.

For the simulation, the Speaker (your instructor) can choose one of two options with regard to allowing amendments to legislation during floor debate. First, the Speaker can assign an open rule to all legislation. This means that any section of the legislation being debated on the floor can be amended by any member of the House. The second option is for the Speaker to call upon the two parties to create a Rules Committee. This optional activity is described below.

Optional Activity: Voting on Rules of Debate

If the Speaker opts to seat a Rules Committee, the majority party should select four members and the minority party should select two members to serve as the Rules Committee for the simulation. This committee will meet after the standing committees have voted their bills out of committee. It is the job of the Rules Committee to set rules of debate—open, closed, or modified—for each item approved by the committees of jurisdiction. The Rules Committee Worksheet that follows contains columns for the bill name or number, the author's name, and the committee of jurisdiction. It also contains columns for the Rules Committee to fill in what rule it is attaching, to explain any modified rule it decides upon, and to record its vote.

During its deliberations concerning which rule it will issue for any item of pending business, the Rules Committee may elect to call witnesses to testify. These witnesses may be the bill's author, the committee chair or ranking member from the committee of jurisdiction, or members of the House leadership. Whether or not the committee elects to call the leaders as witnesses, the members of the Rules Committee should consult with them to ensure that the leadership (especially the leadership of the majority party) is satisfied with the rule that is issued by the committee.

In the event that a Rules Committee is seated, the rules issued by the committee will have to be voted upon and approved by the full House session before debate can proceed on the legislation.

RULES COMMITTEE WORKSHEET (OPTIONAL)

Bill Name/Number	Author	Committee of Jurisdiction	Rule (Circle One)	If Modified, What Can Be Amended?	Vote in Rules Committee
			Open Closed Modified		
			Open Closed Modified		
			Open Closed Modified		
			Open Closed Modified		
			Open Closed Modified		
			Open Closed Modified		
			Open Closed Modified		
			Open Closed Modified		
			Open Closed Modified		
			Open Closed Modified		

SIMULATION EXERCISE:
SECOND PARTY CAUCUSES

Once your legislation has come out of committee, or out of the Rules Committee if your simulated House opts to use one, it will be necessary for your party to hold a second party caucus. (If your party has been meeting regularly outside of the time set aside for the simulation, then this will be simply the latest in a series of party meetings.) The point here is for your party to refine its priorities by considering which legislation was passed through committee. The goal is for your party to develop a list of priorities and to forward it to the Speaker (your instructor) so that he or she can determine, first, the order in which the legislation ought to be scheduled and, second, how much time should be allotted to consider each item. If a Rules Committee was used, the committee may have indicated through its rule a specific number of amendments, and that will need to be taken into consideration during the scheduling process.

When your party meets in this caucus, it will be important to try to reach agreement on which of the items that came out of committee your party believes should be passed, and which it believes should be blocked or defeated. It will be important to assess whether individual members are uncomfortable with any of the bills supported by the party leadership (the last thing that a party wants is for one of its priorities to be challenged by one of its own members). Your party will also probably want to determine which members intend to speak on behalf of, or against, the legislation that is pending. This will expedite the floor debate process. Finally, in this second caucus, the parties will each want to determine who within their party intends to offer amendments to the legislation.

The bottom line is that this party caucus provides a final opportunity for each party to determine its strategy for floor debate. In addition to determining what the party's priorities are, this is a time to determine how best to accomplish those priorities.

FLOOR DEBATE AND VOTING

Once legislation has been approved by committee and scheduled by the Speaker, the members' responsibilities shift. Now, members must persuade their colleagues—many of whom know nothing about the legislative proposal—that the legislation is worthy of approval by the full House. You will need to engage in techniques similar to those you used to persuade your committee colleagues to pass your legislation.

Floor debate in the House is both highly regimented and extremely complicated. Walter Oleszek notes that there are six general steps in the floor debate process:

1. Adoption of the rule granted by the Rules Committee
2. The act of resolving the House into the Committee of the Whole
3. General debate
4. The amending process

5. The motion to recommit

6. Final action by the full House[19]

Of course, it is not practical for the simulated House to follow these steps exactly. For one thing, members of Congress do this for a living—that is, they have far more time to spend on these endeavors than do students in a classroom simulation. Second, the simulation does not allow for motions to recommit (a **motion to recommit** is a motion to send the pending business back to the committee that originally approved it for more study or amendments). Therefore, the rules of procedure for debating legislation in the simulation vary somewhat from the rules of procedure used by the actual United States House of Representatives. Keep in mind, however, that they serve the same purpose. Just as the rules of debate used by the House of Representatives are designed to create a process conducive to the transaction of legislative business, so too are the rules of procedure for the simulated House.

Debate and Voting in the Full House Session

During the full House session, authors of legislation should be prepared to make a brief statement on behalf of their bills, and all members of the House should be prepared to participate fully during the debate over their own legislative proposals and those of their colleagues. If your instructor has chosen to incorporate a Rules Committee, then that committee will set the rules of debate; it will report each rule in the form of a House resolution that will be debated on and approved separate from the legislation itself. If your instructor does not include a Rules Committee in the simulation, then the Speaker will work with the majority and minority leaders to establish the rules of debate for each piece of legislation. In general, floor debate will proceed as follows.

If the Rules Committee was used to draft the rule of debate on the legislation, the first order of business will be to approve the rule. In that event, the majority leader will first need to call up the rule, which should be in the form of a House resolution, before proceeding to debate on the legislation. He or she will do that as follows:

> Mr. Chairman, I call up House Resolution _____, for a period not to exceed _____ minutes, equally divided. For that purpose, I yield _____ minutes to the honorable Minority Leader, and the remainder of my time to the honorable _____, Chairman of the Committee on Rules.

The minority leader will then respond with:

> Mr. Chairman, I yield my time to the honorable _____, Ranking Minority Member on the Committee.

If a Rules Committee was used and multiple rules need to be adopted (that is, one per item of pending business), then all rules will be voted on before proceeding to the Committee of the Whole. This will expedite the simulation's floor procedures. (Please note that this is different from the actual House of Representatives, which votes on the rule for a piece of legislation immediately prior to debating that piece of legislation. The simulation procedure was changed to expedite the process.)

motion to recommit A motion that, if approved, sends the bill back to the committee of jurisdiction. The motion to recommit is a prerogative of the minority party; it is the minority's last opportunity to revise or kill a piece of pending legislation before the vote for final passage. There are two types of motions to recommit: with instructions or without. A motion to recommit with instructions has the effect of returning the legislation to committee for additional processing in accordance with the instructions; a motion to recommit without instructions has the effect of killing the legislation, because it returns the legislation to the committee indefinitely.

If no Rules Committee was used, the steps numbered below should be followed for debating the legislation. The rules of debate for each item of pending business should then be distributed or announced by the Speaker or majority leader before taking up each item of pending business.

1. The Speaker will declare the House resolved into the Committee of the Whole (the Speaker then becomes the chair).

2. The majority leader should seek recognition from the chair and call up whichever bill or resolution he or she wishes to debate, as follows:

   > Mr. Chairman, pursuant to House Rules, I call up the
   > _____ bill to be debated for _____ minutes,
   > equally divided. For that purpose, I yield _____ minutes to the
   > distinguished Minority Leader. I further yield the remainder of my time
   > to the honorable _____, Chairman of the Committee
   > on _____ [committee of jurisdiction for the bill].

3. The minority leader should respond with:

   > Mr. Chairman, I yield my time to the honorable _____,
   > Ranking Minority Member on the Committee.

4. The Committee chairman from the committee of jurisdiction will say:

   > I thank the Majority Leader, and recognize _____,
   > the author of the legislation, for a period of one minute to explain the
   > proposal.

   Note: This time does not count against the majority.

5. The bill/resolution's author now summarizes his or her legislation. During this time, the author should offer any changes to his or her bill. These are considered to be technical corrections, and thus will be considered as part of the original bill.

6. Once the author has summarized his or her bill, the majority **floor leader** announces: "We will now move into a period of general debate." At this point, there are a number of options for how to proceed: (1) The majority floor manager (the chair of the committee of jurisdiction) may debate the measure. (2) The majority floor manager may immediately yield time to another majority member who wishes to debate the measure. If another member debates but does not use all the time allotted to the majority, he or she should yield the remainder of the time back to the majority floor manager, who can then recognize someone else. A combination of options 1 and 2 may also be used.

   Another option is for the majority floor leader to "reserve" his or her time. This means that he or she does not wish to speak on the legislation, or that there is no other member who seeks recognition, but that following debate from the minority, the majority floor manager reserves the right to use the time to respond. This is also perfectly acceptable. However, the total amount of time consumed by the majority party for general debate on the measure cannot exceed the amount of time allotted to the majority party by the majority leader.

7. Once the majority party has consumed all of its time, or has reserved the remainder of its time, the minority floor manager will be recognized by the chair. The minority party has the same options available to it as did the majority party with regard to floor debate. Again, however, the party cannot consume any time above or beyond what was allotted to it by the majority leader.

floor leader On a specific piece of legislation, the person selected from each party to organize the flow of debate. Generally, the majority party's floor leader is the majority leader or the chair of the committee of jurisdiction. The minority party's floor leader is usually the minority leader or the ranking member on the committee of jurisdiction.

8. Debate continues, alternating back and forth between the majority and minority parties, until all time has expired or until there are no more members on either side seeking recognition.

As you think about participating in general debate, you may wish to consider the following tips:

- At any time, a member can rise on a point of "personal privilege" and ask a question of the bill's author. So, if you have a question, you should say: "Mr. Chairman, I rise on a point of personal privilege with a question for the author." The chair will recognize you, and you may ask your question. Note: This does not subtract from the time allowed for debate.

- It is entirely at the discretion of the floor leaders to recognize the floor managers.

- It is entirely at the discretion of the floor managers to recognize members to speak during general debate.

- It is entirely at the discretion of the chair to recognize members to offer amendments.

- Remember: You *are* the member of Congress you are role-playing. So, your positions on legislation should reflect that member's positions. If you are unsure how your member would vote on any given bill, get on the Internet, go to the library, call his or her office—whatever you need to do to play your role appropriately.

- This is politics, not personal. *No* personal attacks will be permitted; the chair has discretion on this point.

- Have fun!

9. Once general debate has concluded on the legislation, the chair will recognize the majority leader, who will state: "Mr. Chairman, pursuant to House rules, we will now move into a period of _____ minutes for the purpose of amending this bill. Time shall be equally divided." The chair will then recognize members offering amendments in the order in which amendments were received, or the order in which members indicate that they wish to offer an amendment.

    9a. The author of the amendment will get one minute to make his or her argument.

    9b. The chair will recognize one person to speak against the amendment for one minute.

    9c. The amendment will be voted upon by the Committee of the Whole.

    9d. This process continues until all time has expired, or until all amendments are disposed of.

10. Once the amending process has been completed, the simulated House will set the bill aside. It will not vote on it, as the Committee of the Whole cannot actually approve legislation. All it can do is amend it to make it acceptable. Only the House of Representatives itself can pass legislation.

11. Once debate on all pending business (or as much of it as can reasonably be concluded in the time allotted) is complete, the Committee of the Whole will dissolve itself back into the House of Representatives. According to Oleszek, this is frequently triggered by the rule attached to the legislation that will require the Committee of the Whole to dissolve at

that point.[20] In the simulated House, the chair will simply call for a return to the House of Representatives.

12. With the Committee of the Whole dissolved and the House back in session, the House will take up each piece of legislation for a straight up-or-down vote. There will be no opportunities for debate. Instead, the Speaker will simply call up each piece of legislation and ask that a roll-call vote be taken on it.

In order to keep track of what happens to each piece of legislation that is debated, you may wish to use the Floor Debate Worksheet on the next page. Keeping track of the fate of each piece of legislation, as well as how you voted on it, may be useful to you as you think about how you will justify your votes to your constituents.

FLOOR DEBATE WORKSHEET

Bill Title	Author	Yea Votes (in favor)	Nay Votes (against)	My Vote (yea or nay)

Optional Activity: Senate Floor Consideration

If your class is large enough, or if there is sufficient time, your instructor may wish to refer the legislation that has passed the House to a simulated Senate chamber. Because the focus of the simulation is on the House of Representatives, this optional Senate exercise is not intended to be as extensive as the House simulation. Nonetheless, if used to supplement the House simulation, this exercise can help clarify the differences in procedures used by the House and the Senate.

If your class is small, each student will need to be reassigned to portray a member of the Senate (a list of all of the senators in the 108th Congress is available at http://www.senate.gov). If your class is large enough, some members of the class could portray senators while others portray House members. For this Senate exercise, there are no committees, as the procedures used by Senate committees vary little from those used by committees in the House. The senators should meet in party conferences (which are the same as House caucuses) for the purposes of identifying their legislative priorities; this can be done either inside or outside of class, depending on the timing of this part of the simulation. As part of these conferences, the majority and minority parties should each select a leader and a floor manager for each piece of legislation.

Following these party conferences, floor debate can proceed. Your instructor will serve as the presiding officer, and the majority and minority leaders will manage the floor debate. Unlike the House of Representatives, the Senate has many fewer rules of debate. The Senate majority leader will ask that the Senate proceed to its first item of business (whatever piece of legislation the leader wishes to call up first). In order to proceed, the leader will ask unanimous consent to call up the legislation, and for the purposes of the simulation, the assumption will be that there is no objection to the unanimous consent request. Once the legislation is called up, the Senate will move directly into a period of debate on the legislation.

During debate in the actual U.S. Senate, no member of the Senate can speak twice on any single piece of legislation according to Rule XIV of the *Standing Rules of the Senate*. However, Rule XIV does not mention for how long a senator may speak when he or she holds the floor. In fact, in the U.S. Senate, any senator may hold the floor for as long as he or she is able to continue speaking. The *filibuster,* or right of unlimited debate, was once described as permitting a member of the Senate to speak until his knee hit the floor— literally, until the senator fell down from sheer exhaustion. For most of the Senate's history, the chamber had no mechanism to cut off a filibuster. However, in 1917 and again in 1975, the Senate adopted amendments that substantively changed Rule XXII, which is known as the Senate **cloture** rule.[21] The cloture procedure permits 16 senators to petition to end debate. Debate will be brought to a halt if 60 senators (three-fifths of the membership) vote to end debate. If fewer than 60 senators vote to end debate, the filibuster continues, and can only be brought to a halt if the filibusterer(s) decide(s) to give up or if the Senate majority leader "pulls the bill down"—decides to end debate on the legislation. Pulling the bill down is tantamount to an admission by the majority party that it does not have the votes or the clout to ensure passage of the legislation.

In this simulated Senate exercise, just as in the real U.S. Senate, any member of the Senate has the right to filibuster. However, also just as in the real Senate,

cloture The mechanism for ending a Senate filibuster.

any senator who engages in a filibuster must be speaking at all times. And, should the other "senators" wish to end debate, they are equally able to use Rule XXII to invoke cloture.

Unlike the House, where the floor managers very actively manage floor debate, in the Senate, debate is managed somewhat by the floor leaders and somewhat by the presiding officer, in large part because of the less regimented nature of Senate debate. The Senate often uses **time agreements**—agreements between the majority and minorities leaders about how long they will permit debate on a piece of legislation. This is similar to the House's use of rules and procedures that require very strict adherence to time constraints.

For this optional exercise, the presiding officer will take on much of the task of managing floor debate. Members seeking recognition should stand and wait to be recognized by the presiding officer (who, again, will be portrayed by your instructor). Upon being asked by the presiding officer "On what point do you rise?" any member of the simulated Senate may seek to do virtually anything by asking for unanimous consent: "Mr. President, I ask unanimous consent to . . ." (in the case of the Senate, the presiding officer is referred to as the president, as the official title of the presiding officer is President, or President Pro Tempore, of the Senate). Debate will continue for as long as members of the Senate continue to seek recognition, provided that the debate conforms to whatever unanimous consent or time agreements the majority and minority party leaders have agreed to ahead of time.

time agreement An agreement between the Senate majority and minority leaders concerning the amount of time that will be spent debating a particular piece of legislation.

Optional Activity: Conference Committees

If your instructor opts to include the Senate activity, it is also possible to simulate the experience of conference committees. The purpose of conference committees in the Congress is to reconcile the differences in legislation passed by the House and the Senate.

Conference committees are temporary joint committees, meaning they are composed of members of both the House and the Senate. Although the process for seating these committees varies by chamber, in both the House and Senate the leadership appoints members of the conference committees, who are called *conferees*. Frequently, the conferees are members of the standing committee that originally had jurisdiction over the legislation. They have expertise in both the general subject matter of the legislation and the specific pieces of legislation being reconciled in the conference committee. As noted in the previous chapter, there is no standard size for conference committees; they may range in size from a mere handful of members from each chamber all the way to 200 or so members. Larger conference committees are generally seated when the legislation's subject matter spans multiple committees of jurisdiction, including omnibus legislation (legislation that is lengthy and addresses multiple subjects). In conference, each chamber gets only one vote. That means that either chamber can effectively prevent the other chamber from exercising its will.

In conference, each chamber attempts to accomplish several goals. The first is to preserve as much as possible of the language and proposals that are chamber-specific. In this sense, each chamber wants to "win" in conference. A competitive spirit does not strictly motivate that desire; rather, conferees recognize that the version of the legislation they are in conference to defend has already been approved by a majority of members of their chamber. Preserving as much of the version their chamber passed as possible is important, because conferees need to ensure that whatever comes out of conference will also be acceptable to a majority of the members of their chamber.

In order to simulate the experience of conference committees, you will need to seat conferees from both the simulated House and the simulated Senate. Different conferees may be seated for different items of legislation, but all members of the simulated House and Senate must be on at least one conference committee. Each conference committee shall have the responsibility to reconcile the differences between the House and Senate versions of legislation passed during the simulation.

COMMUNICATING WITH CONSTITUENTS

Once you have concluded the business of debating and approving legislation on Capitol Hill, your focus will shift homeward. As a "single-minded seeker of reelection," an important part of your job is to make what you do in Washington real to your constituents. This is what Richard Fenno refers to as "home style," or the way that you present yourself to your constituents back home.[22]

Members of Congress have a variety of methods at their disposal for communicating with their constituents. Almost all use their official Web sites to post information that is relevant to their constituents, and many include information on the sites about projects and services they have procured for their constituents. Many members of Congress make frequent trips home as well, to allow them to meet face to face with the residents of their districts. In fact, some members of the House are known as the "Tuesday to Thursday" club because they are only in Washington from Tuesday morning until Thursday night. (Fortunately, the House schedule for voting permits members to keep this sort of schedule.) Some members even sleep in their offices rather than spend the money to rent an apartment or buy a second home.

Of course, members of Congress also take full advantage of their **franking privilege**—their right to send a specified amount of mail using the U.S. Postal Service without having to pay out of pocket for it. They use this privilege to send letters to their constituents in response to constituency requests. Many members also take advantage of the franking privilege to send a periodic newsletter back to their constituents to describe what has taken place on the Hill.

franking privilege The right to send a specified amount of mail without paying out of pocket for it. The member's signature, or frank, on the back of the envelope is sufficient to allow the piece of mail to be delivered.

As part of the simulation, you, too, are expected to communicate with the people who sent you to Washington on their behalf. You are to do this in at least one, and possibly two, ways. First, once floor debate is concluded, you are to draft a newsletter to send to your constituents. That assignment is detailed below. A second method of communicating with your constituents is to create a Web page. The Speaker will tell you whether or not you are to do this, as it may require you to seek the assistance of someone with expertise designing and posting Web pages.

SIMULATION ASSIGNMENT 7:
CONSTITUENCY NEWSLETTER

As the session comes to an end, it will be time to turn your attention to re-election. Although it seems like only yesterday that you were campaigning for your seat in this Congress, it's time to start planning to run again. To that end, it's time to communicate with your constituents about your activities during this session of Congress.

Your assignment is to draft a newsletter to your constituents. The newsletter should be of sufficient length to address the following issues:

- Your legislative activities during this session (committee assignments, activities, cosponsorships of legislation, participation in floor debates, etc.)
- Your success/failure to achieve passage for your legislation, and an explanation of the outcome
- What projects, revenues, and the like you have procured for your district during this session of Congress
- Information about, and justification for, the bills you supported/did not support in this Congress
- What you wish had been/had not been enacted

You can opt to write this as a straightforward letter to your constituents, or you can be creative and write this in newsletter format (most word processing programs provide templates that allow you to do this). In either case, the same rules apply: Your newsletter must be clearly written, free from grammatical and proofreading errors, and must address each of the topics mentioned above. As you begin to draft your newsletter, you should also keep in mind that you most likely will need to provide some background information on each piece of legislation you mention (since your constituents won't know anything about the legislation except what you tell them). You will also want to be explicit about how your legislative activities will benefit your constituents—remember, this is your opportunity to prove to your constituents that you have served them well.

OPTIONAL SIMULATION ASSIGNMENT:
MEMBER WEB PAGE

As noted above, every member of Congress has at least a basic Web page that he or she uses to present his or her Washington, DC, activities to the constituents he or she represents. Your assignment is to create a Web site that allows you, as a member of Congress, to present yourself to your constituents. Your Web page must include the following elements:

- A disclaimer at the top that states: "This is not the official Web site for [name of member]. His/Her official Web site can be found at http://www.house.gov. This site is intended for use in a classroom simulation ONLY. Its contents do not reflect the views of [the name of the member you're portraying], [your college's name], or [your instructor's name].

- A copy of your member profile. You may choose to post it as a single document or to break it up into smaller sections to be posted under specific headings (for example: Personal Information, District Information, etc.).
- Creativity! Add a digital photo of yourself, a picture of the Congress, a cool background, or other creative details.

A variety of computer software programs can assist you with Web page design. In addition, you may wish to check out several Web pages belonging to actual members of Congress at http://www.house.gov and http://www.senate.gov to get ideas for yours. Also, you will need to take care to avoid downloading copyrighted material. Use only images/text that are in the public domain, and always cite your source (yes, even on your Web site!) for any information you have downloaded.

CONCLUSION

By this point, you may be so tired of the Congress that you are simply relieved that the simulation is over. You have drafted and redrafted legislation, listened to countless proposals from your colleagues, and spent a lot of time considering how to make changes to legislation to adapt and improve it. If the simulation has worked well, you will have discovered the difficulty of drafting legislation, the difficulty of evaluating and amending other members' legislation, and the frustration of seeing your legislation changed. A colleague who went too far in criticizing your legislation may have angered you. You may have felt the anguish of watching helplessly as your colleagues—your friends—ensured that the legislation never saw the light of day. You will likely have felt frustration at the regimented nature of the process, at how thickheaded your colleagues were about the point of your legislation, and at how slow and tedious the legislative process can be.

On the other hand, you may have felt the adrenaline rush that comes from debating your colleagues. You may have felt exhilarated as the legislation you championed passed on the floor of the House or the Senate. You may have felt the satisfaction of seeing the work you did taken seriously by your colleagues. And you may have felt supported by the efforts of your colleagues who agreed with you and worked with you to help you achieve your goals.

If you are feeling these things at the end of the simulation, then the simulation worked. You experienced the things that real-life members of Congress experience on a daily basis. Most members will tell you that the feelings of satisfaction they get from serving not only their constituents but also their country are without equal. They typically enjoy bonds of friendship, collegiality, and camaraderie with their fellow members of Congress. They are often hailed as heroes for the legislation they champion that helps to make people's lives better. But members of Congress are also forced to deal with difficult colleagues, difficult legislative proposals, and the time-consuming nature of the legislative process. They must grapple with the competing demands of their constituents, their colleagues, their political party, and their own consciences. Many, especially those who serve in the House of Representatives, maintain two households, and most see very little of their families when the Congress is in session.

They endure these difficulties all the while knowing that the institution of the Congress is hated by a large segment of the American public. But in the end, most members of Congress are there because they know that their presence and their hard work do, in most cases, lead to better public policies. They derive tremendous satisfaction from knowing that they are both serving their country and making a difference in people's lives.

Although you did not have to deal with real live constituents, the burdens of a family, two households, or raising money for the next election cycle, you did get a taste of much of the daily activity of a member of Congress. With any luck, you have also learned a lot about the way the Congress works.

4

Resources for Future Study

Literally thousands of texts have been written about the United States Congress. These range from texts that describe the legislative process, to biographies of members of Congress, to historical treatments of the institution, to discussions of particular legislative proposals that have been debated and approved by the Congress. For a student confronted with the need to conduct research on the process, it can be a daunting task to sift through all of these texts. The bibliography that follows is an attempt to make students aware of just a fraction of the resources available. It should not be treated as a comprehensive listing of all the resources that exist. Moreover, it does not include journal or popular press articles, which will likely also prove valuable to your research efforts.

BIOGRAPHIES/AUTOBIOGRAPHIES
OF MEMBERS OF CONGRESS

Barnard, Harry. 2002. *Independent Man: The Life of Senator James Couzens.* Detroit, MI: Wayne State University Press.

Biggs, Jeffrey, and Thomas Foley. 1999. *Honor in the House: Speaker Tom Foley.* Pullman: Washington State University Press.

Bradley, Bill. 1997. *Time Present, Time Past: A Memoir.* New York: Vintage Books.

Caro, Robert A. 2002. *The Years of Lyndon Johnson, Master of the Senate.* New York: Alfred A. Knopf.

Dirksen, Edward McKinley. 1998. *The Education of a Senator.* Urbana: University of Illinois Press.

Drew, Elizabeth. 2002. *Citizen McCain*. New York: Simon and Schuster.

Farrell, John A. 2001. *Tip O'Neill and the Democratic Century.* Boston: Little, Brown.

Frist, William A., and J. Lee Annis. 2002. *Tennessee Senators 1911–2001: Portraits of Leadership in a Century of Change.* Lanham, MD: Madison Books.

Hatch, Orrin. 2002. *Square Peg: Confessions of a Citizen Senator.* New York: Basic Books.

Hodgson, Godfrey. 2000. *The Gentleman from New York: Daniel Patrick Moynihan—A Biography.* Chicago: Houghton Mifflin.

Jeffords, James M. 2001. *My Declaration of Independence.* New York: Simon and Schuster.

Kerrey, Bob. 2002. *When I Was a Young Man.* New York: Harcourt Books.

Lamb, Karl A. 1998. *Reasonable Disagreement: Two U.S. Senators and the Choices That They Make.* New York: Garland.

McCain, John. 2001. *Faith of My Fathers.* New York: Random House.

Merriner, James L. 1999. *Mr. Chairman: Power in Dan Rostenkowski's America.* Carbondale: Southern Illinois University Press.

Mikulski, Barbara, ed. 2001. *Nine and Counting: The Women of the Senate.* New York: Harper Perennial.

O'Neill, Tip (with Gary Hymel). 1995. *All Politics Is Local: And Other Rules of the Game.* Avon, MA: Adams Media Corporation.

Ornstein, Norman J. 1997. *Lessons and Legacies: Farewell Addresses from the Senate.* Reading, MA: Addison Wesley.

Rogers, Mary Beth. 2000. *Barbara Jordan: American Hero.* New York: Bantam Doubleday Dell.

Rudman, Warren B. 1996. *Combat: Twelve Years in the U.S. Senate.* New York: Random House.

Sanders, Bernard (with Huck Gutman). 1998. *Outsider in the House.* New York: Verso Books.

Schroeder, Patricia. 1999. *24 Years of House Work and the Place Is Still a Mess: My Life in Politics.* Kansas City: Andrews McMeel Universal.

Vistica, Gregory. 2003. *The Education of Lieutenant Kerrey.* New York: Thomas Dunne.

Wellstone, Paul David. 2001. *The Conscience of a Liberal: Reclaiming the Compassionate Agenda.* New York: Random House.

West, Darrell M. 2000. *Patrick Kennedy: The Rise to Power.* Upper Saddle River, NJ: Prentice Hall College Division.

BOOKS ABOUT HOW CONGRESS WORKS

Baker, Ross K. 2001. *House and Senate,* 3d ed. New York: W. W. Norton.

Brown, Sherrod. 1999. *Congress from the Inside: Observations from the Majority and Minority.* Kent, OH: Kent State University Press.

Editors of Congressional Quarterly. 1998. *How Congress Works.* Washington, DC: Congressional Quarterly Press.

Frey, Lou, and Michael T. Hayes, eds. 2001. *Inside the House: Former Members Reveal How the Congress Really Works.* Lanham, MD: University Press of America.

Greenberg, Ellen House. 1996. *The House and Senate Explained: The People's Guide to Congress.* New York: W. W. Norton.

Kravitz, Walter. 2001. *American Congressional Dictionary.* Washington, DC: Congressional Quarterly Press.

Price, David Eugene. 2000. *The Congressional Experience.* Boulder, CO: Westview Press.

Silverberg, David. 2002. *Congress for Dummies.* Indianapolis: Wiley .

SCHOLARLY BOOKS ABOUT THE CONGRESS AND THE LEGISLATIVE PROCESS

Bell, Lauren Cohen. 2002. *Warring Factions: Interest Groups, Money, and the New Politics of Senate Confirmation.* Columbus: Ohio State University Press.

Binder, Sarah A., and Stephen S. Smith. 1997. *Politics or Principle: Filibustering in the U.S. Senate.* Washington, DC: Brookings Institution Press.

Elving, Ronald D. 1996. *Conflict and Compromise: How Congress Makes the Law.* New York: Touchstone Books.

Oleszek, Walter J. 2001. *Congressional Procedures and the Policy Process,* 5th ed. Washington, DC: Congressional Quarterly Press.

Redmond, Eric. 2001. *The Dance of Legislation: An Insider's Account of the Workings of the U.S. Senate.* Seattle: University of Washington Press.

Ripley, Randall. 1988. *Congress: Process and Policy.* New York: W.W. Norton.

Rosenthal, Cindy Simon. 2002. *Women Transforming Congress.* Norman: University of Oklahoma Press.

Sinclair, Barbara. 2000. *Unorthodox Lawmaking: New Legislative Processes in the U.S. Congress,* 2d ed. Washington, DC: Congressional Quarterly Press.

Swers, Michele. 2002. *The Difference Women Make.* Chicago: University of Chicago Press.

Notes

CHAPTER 1

1. George Galloway, *History of the United States House of Representatives* (Washington, DC: Government Printing Office, 1965).

2. Ross K. Baker, *House and Senate,* 3d ed. (New York: W. W. Norton, 2001), 38–9.

3. James Sterling Young, *The Washington Community 1800–1828* (New Haven, CT: Yale University Press, 1966).

4. Ibid.

5. Ibid.

6. Ibid.

7. Young, 13.

8. Donald Matthews, *U.S. Senators and Their World* (New York: W. W. Norton, 1973).

CHAPTER 2

1. *Standing Rules of the Senate* (Washington, DC: Government Printing Office, 1990).

2. Walter J. Oleszek, *Congressional Procedures and the Policy Process,* 4th ed. (Washington, DC: Congressional Quarterly Press, 2001), 339–40.

3. Ibid.

4. Christopher J. Deering and Steven S. Smith, *Committees in Congress,* 3d ed. (Washington, DC: Congressional Quarterly Press, 1997), 11–12.

5. U.S. House of Representatives Committee on Rules, *A History of the Committee on Rules* (Washington, DC: Government Printing Office, 1981), 14.

6. Roger H. Davidson and Walter J. Oleszek, *Congress and Its Members,* 8th ed. (Washington, DC: Congressional Quarterly Press, 2002), 243.

7. Oleszek, 157.

8. House Rule XIII.

9. Oleszek, 112.

10. Mary E. Mulvihill, Paul Rundquist, Judy Schneider, and Lorraine H. Tong, "House and Senate Rules of Procedure: A Comparison," *CRS Report for Congress* (Washington, DC: Library of Congress, April 7, 1999), 3; Oleszek.

11. Mulvihill et al., 3.

12. Mulvihill et al., 5.

13. Barbara Sinclair, *Unorthodox Lawmaking: New Legislative Processes in the U.S. Congress,* 2d ed. (Washington, DC: Congressional Quarterly Press, 2000), 60.

14. Stephen E. Frantzich and Stephen E. Schier, *Congress: Games and Strategies* (Madison, WI: Brown and Benchmark, 1994), 127.

15. Ross K. Baker, *House and Senate,* 3d ed. (New York: W. W. Norton, 2001), 67.

16. Norman Ornstein, Thomas Mann, and Michael Malbin, *Vital Statistics on Congress, 2001–2002* (Washington, DC: Congressional Quarterly Press, 2002).

17. As quoted in Baker, 100.

18. Interview by author, August 2000. The senator requested anonymity at the time of the interview.

19. Baker, 237.

20. L. Marvin Overby and Lauren Cohen Bell, *Rational Behavior or the Norm of Cooperation? Filibustering Behavior Among Retiring Senators* (paper presented at the annual meeting of the American Political Science Association, Boston, August 29–September 1, 2002).

21. Sinclair.

22. Sinclair, 71.

23. Glen S. Krutz, *Hitching a Ride: Omnibus Legislating in the U.S. Congress* (Columbus, OH: Ohio State University Press, 2001).

CHAPTER 3

1. David Mayhew, *Congress: The Electoral Connection* (New Haven, CT: Yale University Press, 1974).

2. Gary C. Jacobson and Samuel Kernell, "Strategic Politicians" (excerpt from *Strategy and Choice in Congressional Elections,* 2d ed., 1983), in *Classics in Congressional Politics,* edited by Herbert F. Weisberg, Eric S. Heberlig, and Lisa M. Campoli (New York: Addison, Wesley, Longman, 1999).

3. Thomas A. Kazee, ed., *Who Runs for Congress: Ambition, Context, and Candidate Emergence* (Washington, DC: Congressional Quarterly Press, 1994), 175.

4. Ibid.

5. Richard F. Fenno, Jr., *Home Style: House Members in their Districts* (Glenview, IL: Scott Foresman, 1978); John R. Hibbing, *Congressional Careers: Contours of Life in the U.S. House of Representatives* (Chapel Hill: University of North Carolina Press, 1991).

6. Mildred Amer, "Membership of the 108th Congress: A Profile," CRS Report for Congress (Washington, DC: Congressional Research Service, May 8, 2003), 1.

7. Ibid.

8. Ibid., 2.

9. Ibid., 3.

10. Ibid.

11. Ibid.

12. United States House of Representatives Democratic Caucus, "What Is the Democratic Caucus?" Available online: http://dcaucusweb.house.gov/about/what_is.asp (accessed December 30, 2002).

13. United States Senate Republican Conference, "About the Senate Republican Conference." Available online: http://www.senate.gov/~src/about/index.cfm (accessed December 30, 2002).

14. United States House of Representatives, Office of Legislative Counsel, "About HOLC." Available online: http://legcoun.house.gov/about.html (accessed December 13, 2002).

15. Ibid.

16. Resume of Congressional Activity, years indicated.

17. Roger H. Davidson and Walter J. Oleszek, *Congress and Its Members,* 8th ed. (Washington, DC: Congressional Quarterly Press, 2002); Richard F. Fenno, *Congressmen in Committees* (Boston: Little, Brown, 1973); Christopher J. Deering and Steven S. Smith, *Committees in Congress,* 3d ed. (Washington, DC: Congressional Quarterly Press, 1997).

18. *Congress at Your Fingertips* (Washington, DC: Capitol Advantage, 2003).

19. Oleszek, 150.

20. Oleszek, 172.

21. Congressional Research Service, *Senate Cloture Rule: Limitation of Debate in the Congress of the United States* and *Legislative History of Paragraph 2 of Rule XXII of the Standing Rules of the United States Senate (Cloture Rule),* printed for the United States Senate Committee on Rules and Administration (Washington, DC: U.S. Government Printing Office, 1985).

22. Fenno, *Home Style.*

References

Amer, Mildred. 2003. "Membership of the 108th Congress: A Profile." CRS Report for Congress, May 8, 2003. Washington, DC: Congressional Research Service.

Baker, Ross K. 2001. *House and Senate,* 3d ed. New York: W. W. Norton.

Barone, Michael, Richard E. Cohen, and Charles E. Cook, Jr. 2002. *The Almanac of American Politics.* Washington, DC: National Journal Group.

Congress at Your Fingertips. 2002. Washington, DC: Capitol Advantage.

Congressional Research Service. 1985. *Senate Cloture Rule: Limitation of Debate in the Congress of the United States* and *Legislative History of Paragraph 2 of Rule XXII of the Standing Rules of the United States Senate (Cloture Rule).* Printed for the United States Senate Committee on Rules and Administration. Washington, DC: U.S. Government Printing Office.

Davidson, Roger H., and Walter J. Oleszek. 2002. *Congress and Its Members,* 8th ed. Washington, DC: Congressional Quarterly Press.

Deering, Christopher J., and Steven S. Smith. 1997. *Committees in Congress,* 3d ed. Washington, DC: Congressional Quarterly Press.

Fenno, Richard F., Jr. 1973. *Congressmen in Committees.* Boston: Little, Brown.

———. 1978. *Home Style: House Members in their Districts.* Glenview, IL: Scott Foresman.

Frantzich, Stephen E., and Stephen E. Schier. 1994. *Congress: Games and Strategies.* Madison, WI: Brown and Benchmark.

Galloway, George. 1965. *History of the United States House of Representatives.* Washington, DC: U.S. Government Printing Office.

Hibbing, John R. 1991. *Congressional Careers: Contours of Life in the U.S. House of Representatives.* Chapel Hill: University of North Carolina Press.

Jacobson, Gary C., and Samuel Kernell. 1999. "Strategic Politicians" (excerpt from *Strategy and Choice in Congressional Elections,* 2d ed., 1983). In *Classics in Congressional Politics,* edited by Herbert F. Weisberg, Eric S. Heberlig, and Lisa M. Campoli. New York: Addison, Wesley, Longman.

Kazee, Thomas A., ed. 1994. *Who Runs for Congress: Ambition, Context, and Candidate Emergence.* Washington, DC: Congressional Quarterly Press.

Krutz, Glen S. 2001. *Hitching a Ride: Omnibus Legislating in the U.S. Congress.* Columbus: Ohio State University Press.

Matthews, Donald. 1973. *U.S. Senators and Their World.* New York: W. W. Norton.

Mayhew, David. 1974. *Congress: The Electoral Connection.* New Haven, CT: Yale University Press.

Mulvihill, Mary E., Paul Rundquist, Judy Schneider, and Lorraine H. Tong. 1999. "House and Senate Rules of Procedure: A Comparison." CRS Report for Congress, April 7, 1999. Washington, DC: Library of Congress.

Nutting, Brian, and H. Amy Stern, eds. 2002. *Politics in America.* Washington, DC: Congressional Quarterly Press.

Office of Legislative Counsel, United States House of Representatives. 2002. "About HOLC." Available online: http://legcoun.house.gov/about.html (accessed December 13, 2002).

Oleszek, Walter J. 2001. *Congressional Procedures and the Policy Process.* Washington, DC: Congressional Quarterly Press.

Ornstein, Norman, Thomas Mann, and Michael Malbin. 2002. *Vital Statistics on Congress, 2001–2002.* Washington, DC: Congressional Quarterly Press.

Overby, L. Marvin, and Lauren Cohen Bell. 2002. *Rational Behavior or the Norm of Cooperation? Filibustering Behavior Among Retiring Senators.* Paper presented at the annual meeting of the American Political Science Association, Boston.

Rules of the House of Representatives. 2000. Washington, DC: U.S. Government Printing Office.

Sinclair, Barbara. 2000. *Unorthodox Lawmaking: New Legislative Processes in the U.S. Congress,* 2d ed. Washington, DC: Congressional Quarterly Press.

Standing Rules of the Senate. 1990. Washington, DC: U.S. Government Printing Office.

———. 2000. Washington, DC: U.S. Government Printing Office.

United States House of Representatives Democratic Caucus. 2002. "What Is the Democratic Caucus?" Available online: http://dcaucusweb.house.gov/about/what_is.asp (accessed December 30, 2002).

United States House of Representatives Committee on Rules. 1981. *A History of the Committee on Rules.* Washington, DC: U.S. Government Printing Office.

United States Senate Republican Conference. 2002. "About the Senate Republican Conference." Available online: http://www.senate.gov/~src/about/index.cfm (accessed December 30, 2002).

Williams, Krissah. 2002. "Long Hours, Low Pay: The Thrill of It All: Job Seekers to Converge on Capitol Hill, Compete to Join Congressional Staffs." *Washington Post,* December 29, p. K1.

Young, James Sterling. 1966. *The Washington Community 1800–1828.* New Haven, CT: Yale University Press.

Appendix I
Sample Bills/Resolutions*

106th CONGRESS
2d Session
H. R. 4228

To amend the North Korea Threat Reduction Act of 1999 to enhance congressional oversight of nuclear transfers to North Korea, and for other purposes.

IN THE HOUSE OF REPRESENTATIVES
April 11, 2000

Mr. **Gilman** (for himself, Mr. **Markey**, Mr. **Bereuter**, Mr. **Kucinich**, and Mr. **Cox**) introduced the following bill; which was referred to the Committee on International Relations, and in addition to the Committee on Rules, for a period to be subsequently determined by the Speaker, in each case for consideration of such provisions as fall within the jurisdiction of the committee concerned

---

A BILL

To amend the North Korea Threat Reduction Act of 1999 to enhance congressional oversight of nuclear transfers to North Korea, and for other purposes.

*The sample bills and resolutions in this appendix, as well as thousands of others, can be located using the Congress's official Web site, http://thomas.loc.gov.

Be it enacted by the Senate and House of Representatives of the United States of America in Congress assembled,

SECTION 1. SHORT TITLE.

This Act may be cited as the "Congressional Oversight of Nuclear Transfers to North Korea Act of 2000."

SEC. 2. ENHANCEMENT OF CONGRESSIONAL OVERSIGHT OF NUCLEAR TRANSFERS TO NORTH KOREA.

(a) Establishing Requirement for Congressional Action by Joint Resolution.—The North Korea Threat Reduction Act of 1999 (subtitle B of title VIII of division A of H.R. 3427, as enacted into law by section 1000(a)(7) of Public Law 106-113, and as contained in appendix G to such Public Law) is amended in section 822(a)—

> (1) by redesignating paragraphs (1) through (7) as subparagraphs (A) through (G), respectively, and by indenting each such subparagraph 2 ems to the right;

> (2) by striking "until the President" and inserting "until—

>> "(1) the President"; and

> (3) at the end of subparagraph (G) (as redesignated in paragraph (1)) by striking the period and inserting "; and

>> "(2) a joint resolution described in section 823 is enacted into law pursuant to the provisions of such section." (b) Description and Procedures for Joint Resolution.—The North Korea Threat Reduction Act of 1999 is amended—

> (1) by redesignating section 823 as section 824; and

> (2) by inserting after section 822 the following new section:

"SEC. 823. JOINT RESOLUTION PURSUANT TO SECTION 822(A)(2).

"(a) In General.—For purposes of section 822(a)(2), the term 'joint resolution' means only a joint resolution of the 2 Houses of Congress—"

> "(1) the matter after the resolving clause of which is as follows: 'That the Congress hereby concurs in the determination and report of the President relating to compliance by North Korea with certain international obligations transmitted pursuant to section 822(a)(1) of the North Korea Threat Reduction Act of 1999.';

> "(2) which does not have a preamble; and

"(3) the title of which is as follows: 'Joint Resolution relating to compliance by North Korea with certain international obligations pursuant to the North Korea Threat Reduction Act of 1999.'

"(b) Congressional Review Procedures.—Any joint resolution described in subsection (a) shall be considered in the House of Representatives and the Senate in accordance with the provisions of subsections a. through h. of section 130 of the Atomic Energy Act of 1954, except that—

"(1) the forty-five days of continuous session of Congress referred to in subsection a. of section 130 of the Atomic Energy Act of 1954 shall commence on the date on which the President transmits to the Committee on International Relations of the House of Representatives and the Committee on Foreign Relations of the Senate the determination and report referred to in section 822(a)(1);

"(2) paragraph (3) of subsection d. of such section shall not apply;

"(3) the term 'resolution' or 'concurrent resolution' in subsections a. through h. of such section shall be deemed to refer to a joint resolution described in subsection (a); and

"(4) notwithstanding subsection f. of such section, the text of the resolution described in subsection f. of such section shall be deemed to be the text of the resolution described in subsection (a)."

SEC. 3. EXPANSION OF RESTRICTIONS ON NUCLEAR COOPERATION WITH NORTH KOREA.

Section 822(a) of the North Korea Threat Reduction Act of 1999 is amended by striking "such agreement," both places it appears and inserting in both places "such agreement (or that are controlled under the Export Trigger List of the Nuclear Suppliers Group)."

106th CONGRESS
1st Session
H. J. RES. 62

To grant the consent of Congress to the boundary change between Georgia and South Carolina.

IN THE HOUSE OF REPRESENTATIVES

July 22, 1999

Mr. **Linder** (for himself, Mr. **Kingston,** and Mr. **Spence**) introduced the following joint resolution; which was referred to the Committee on the Judiciary

September 8, 1999

Committed to the Committee of the Whole House on the State of the Union and ordered to be printed

---

JOINT RESOLUTION

To grant the consent of Congress to the boundary change between Georgia and South Carolina.

Resolved by the Senate and House of Representatives of the United States of America in Congress assembled,

SECTION 1. CONSENT OF CONGRESS.

(a) In General.—The consent of Congress is given to the establishment of the boundary between the States of Georgia and South Carolina.

(b) New Boundary.—The boundary referred to in subsection (a) is the boundary—

(1) agreed to by the State of Georgia in Act Number 1044 (S.B. No. 572) approved by the Governor on April 5, 1994, and agreed to by the State of South Carolina in Act Number 375 (S.B. No. 1315) approved by the Governor on May 29, 1996;

(2) agreed to by the State of Georgia in Act Number 1044 (S.B. No. 572) approved by the Governor on April 5, 1994, and agreed to by the State of South Carolina in an Act approved by its Governor not later than 5 years after the date of the enactment of this joint resolution;

(3) agreed to by the State of South Carolina in Act Number 375 (S.B. No. 1315) approved by the Governor on May 29, 1996, and agreed to

by the State of Georgia in an Act approved by its Governor not later than 5 years after the date of the enactment of this joint resolution; or

(4) agreed to by the States of Georgia and South Carolina in Acts approved by each of their Governors not later than 5 years after the date of enactment of this joint resolution.

(c) Compact.—The Acts referred to in subsection (b) are recognized by Congress as an interstate compact pursuant to section 10 of article I of the United States Constitution.

106th CONGRESS
1st Session
H. CON. RES. 131

Condemning Palestinian efforts to revive the original Palestine partition plan of November 29, 1947, and condemning the United Nations Commission on Human Rights for its April 27, 1999, resolution endorsing Palestinian self-determination on the basis of the original Palestine partition plan.

IN THE HOUSE OF REPRESENTATIVES

June 10, 1999

Mr. **Nadler** (for himself, Ms. **Ros-Lehtinen**, Mr. **Engel**, Mr. **Gilman**, Mr. **McNulty**, Mr. **Pallone**, and Mr. **Weiner**) submitted the following concurrent resolution; which was referred to the Committee on International Relations

---

CONCURRENT RESOLUTION

Condemning Palestinian efforts to revive the original Palestine partition plan of November 29, 1947, and condemning the United Nations Commission on Human Rights for its April 27, 1999, resolution endorsing Palestinian self-determination on the basis of the original Palestine partition plan.

Whereas United Nations General Assembly Resolution 181, which called for the partition of the British-ruled Palestine Mandate into a Jewish state and an Arab state, was declared null and void on November 29, 1947, by the Arab states and the Palestinians, who included the rejection of Resolution 181 as a formal justification for the May 1948, invasion of the newly declared State of Israel by the armies of 5 Arab states;

Whereas the armistice agreements between Israel and Egypt, Lebanon, Syria, and Transjordan in 1949 made no mention of United Nations General Assembly Resolution 181, and the United Nations Security Council made no reference to United Nations General Assembly Resolution 181 in its Resolution 73 on August 11, 1949, which endorsed the armistice;

Whereas in 1967 and 1973 the United Nations adopted Security Council Resolutions 242 and 338, respectively, which call for the withdrawal of Israel from territory occupied in 1967 and 1973 in exchange for the creation of secure and recognized boundaries for Israel and for political recognition of Israel's sovereignty;

Whereas Security Council Resolutions 242 and 338 have served as the framework for all negotiations between Israel, Palestinian representatives, and

Arab states for 30 years, including the 1991 Madrid Peace Conference and the ongoing Oslo peace process, and serve as the agreed basis for impending Final Status Negotiations;

Whereas senior Palestinian officials have recently resurrected United Nations General Assembly Resolution 181 through official statements and a March 25, 1999, letter from the Palestine Liberation Organization Permanent Observer to the United Nations Secretary-General contending that the State of Israel must withdraw to the borders outlined in United Nations General Assembly Resolution 181, and accept Jerusalem as a "corpus separatum" to be placed under United Nations control as outlined in United Nations General Assembly Resolution 181; and

Whereas in its April 27, 1999, resolution, the United Nations Commission on Human Rights asserted that Israeli-Palestinian peace negotiations be based on United Nations General Assembly Resolution 181:

Now, therefore, be it Resolved by the House of Representatives (the Senate concurring),
That the Congress—

(1) condemns Palestinian efforts to circumvent United Nations Security Council Resolutions 242 and 338, as well as violate the Oslo peace process, by attempting to revive United Nations General Assembly Resolution 181, thereby placing the entire Israeli-Palestinian peace process at risk;

(2) condemns the United Nations Commission on Human Rights for voting to formally endorse United Nations General Assembly Resolution 181 as the basis for the future of Palestinian self-determination;

(3) reiterates that any just and final peace agreement regarding the final status of the territory controlled by the Palestinians can only be determined through direct negotiations and agreement between the State of Israel and the Palestinian Liberation Organization;

(4) reiterates its continued unequivocal support for the security and well-being of the State of Israel, and of the Oslo peace process based on United Nations Security Council Resolutions 242 and 338; and

(5) calls for the President of the United States to declare that—

(A) it is the policy of the United States that United Nations General Assembly Resolution 181 of 1947 is null and void;

(B) all negotiations between Israel and the Palestinians must be based on United Nations Security Council Resolutions 242 and 338; and

(C) the United States regards any attempt by the Palestinians, the United Nations, or any entity to resurrect United Nations General Assembly Resolution 181 as a basis for negotiations, or for any international decision, as an attempt to sabotage the prospects for a successful peace agreement in the Middle East.

H. Res. 151

In the House of Representatives, U.S.,

April 28, 1999

Resolved, That upon the adoption of this resolution it shall be in order to debate the deployment of United States Armed Forces in and around the territory of the Federal Republic of Yugoslavia for one hour equally divided and controlled among the chairmen and ranking minority members of the Committees on International Relations and Armed Services.

Sec. 2. After debate pursuant to the first section of this resolution, it shall be in order without intervention of the question of consideration to consider in the House the bill (H.R. 1569) to prohibit the use of funds appropriated to the Department of Defense from being used for the deployment of ground elements of the United States Armed Forces in the Federal Republic of Yugoslavia unless that deployment is specifically authorized by law. The bill shall be considered as read for amendment. The previous question shall be considered as ordered on the bill to final passage without intervening motion except: (1) one hour of debate equally divided and controlled by the chairman and ranking minority member of the Committee on Armed Services; and (2) one motion to recommit.

Sec. 3. After disposition of H.R. 1569, it shall be in order without intervention of any point of order or the question of consideration to consider in the House the concurrent resolution (H. Con. Res. 82) directing the President, pursuant to section 5(c) of the War Powers Resolution, to remove United States Armed Forces from their positions in connection with the present operations against the Federal Republic of Yugoslavia. The concurrent resolution shall be considered as read for amendment. The concurrent resolution shall be debatable for one hour equally divided and controlled by the chairman and ranking minority member of the Committee on International Relations. The previous question shall be considered as ordered on the concurrent resolution to final adoption without intervening motion.

Sec. 4. After disposition of H. Con. Res. 82, it shall be in order without intervention of any point of order or the question of consideration to consider in the House the joint resolution (H.J. Res. 44) declaring a state of war between the United States and the Government of the Federal Republic of Yugoslavia. The joint resolution shall be considered as read for amendment. The previous question shall be considered as ordered on the joint resolution to final passage without intervening motion except: (1) one hour of debate equally divided and controlled by the chairman and ranking minority member of the Committee on International Relations; and (2) one motion to recommit.

Sec. 5. After disposition of H.J. Res. 44, it shall be in order on the same legislative day without intervention of the question of consideration to consider in the House the concurrent resolution (S. Con. Res. 21) authorizing the President of the United States to conduct military air operations and missile strikes against the Federal Republic of Yugoslavia (Serbia and Montenegro), if called up by Representative Gejdenson of Connecticut or his designee. The concurrent resolution shall be considered as read for amendment. The concurrent resolution shall be debatable for one hour equally divided and controlled by the chairman and ranking minority member of the Committee on International Relations. The previous question shall be considered as ordered on the concurrent resolution to final adoption without intervening motion.

Attest:

Clerk.

Appendix II
Sample Dear Colleague
Letters*

U.S. HOUSE OF REPRESENTATIVES

October 1, 2002

Support Working Americans and Procedural Fairness

Oppose H.R. 5469!

Dear Colleague:

As you may know, the House will be considering H.R. 5469 under suspension of the rules today on the House floor. We urge you to oppose this bill because it hurts everyday, working Americans and has not been vetted through the proper procedure. That is why the bill is opposed by artist groups including: the AFL-CIO, the American Federation of Musicians, the American Federation of Television and Radio Artists, the National Academy of Recording Arts & Sciences, and the Recording Artist Coalition.

First, the proposed legislation prevents artists, musicians, and vocalists from being paid by Internet companies for Internet broadcasts of their music. The Copyright Office ruled this past Summer that the Internet companies should pay these creators of music 0.07¢ per song per listener for broadcasts

---

*Dear Colleague letters can be found online at most House and Senate committee Web sites at http://www.house.gov or http://www.senate.gov. The Dear Colleague letters here were written by the members whose names appear at the end of each letter and are reproduced verbatim, except where the members reference specific congressional staff members. In those cases, the names and contact information for the particular congressional staffers have been removed.

between October 1998 and October 2002 (the Office must set rates for every two-year period). Under the law, the artists would get 45% of that, and the vocalists and musicians each would receive 2.5%. The payments are due on October 20, 2002. The Internet companies and the creators are appealing the rate decision in the Federal courts. At the same time, the Internet companies want Congress to pass this bill, which says the creators would receive no royalty payments for at least six months. This means the creators receive no income for the past four years that the Internet companies were building their businesses on other people's creativity. Keep in mind, these are the same Internet companies that manage to find money for computers, high-speed Internet connections, servers, and the other equipment they need for their businesses.

Moreover, the bill helps not only the smallest, non-profit webcaster but also corporate, media, and technology giants. You may hear that this legislation is good for community-based and school-based webcasters. In reality, this bill is an end-of-session present to billion dollar conglomerates that can easily afford to pay for the music they want to sell, just as Ford pays for steel.

Second, bringing this legislation to the floor under suspension violates virtually every known procedure in the House. The bill was introduced only this past Thursday. There have been no hearings or markups in Committee, and we are voting on it today, the next business day after it was introduced. On top of that, it is being brought up under suspension so members have absolutely no opportunity to offer amendments to fix the problems it clearly has.

We urge you to vote "NO" on this anti-working American, unfair bill.

Sincerely,

Richard A. Gephardt   John Conyers, Jr.   Howard L. Berman
Democratic Leader   Ranking Member   Ranking Member
                            Committee on the   Subcomm. on Courts,
                                Judiciary   the Internet, and
                                                       Intellectual Property

SOURCE: http://www.house.gov/judiciary_democrats/hr5469gendc10102.pdf

Protect Landowners and Species
Co-Sponsor the Endangered Species
Recovery Act

January 25, 1999

Dear Colleague:

Whether you are a new member, or have been in Congress for many years, we have all heard the complaints about the Endangered Species Act. The most common complaint, and the one that seems to be shared by friends and foes of the Act alike, is that while species continue to be listed, few ever are recovered and ESA regulations on landowners never go away.

To address these concerns and more effectively protect both species and landowners, I introduced the Endangered Species Recovery Act (ESRA) in the last Congress. That bill, which I plan to re-introduce in the next few weeks, had more than 100 co-sponsors and was designed to recover endangered species **by implementing the recommendations of the National Academy of Sciences**. These recommendations included improving the scientific basis for listing species and other decisions; using independent scientists to peer review large-scale habitat conservation plans; and allowing scientists, not politicians, to identify what is needed to recover and de-list species.

ESRA's goal is to recover and delist endangered and threatened species. Currently, permits for activities that can damage species habitat are granted based on a determination of whether they move a species closer to extinction, not by whether they will affect the ability to recover species. As a result, very few species have been recovered and landowners face never-ending ESA regulation. ESRA would require recovery to be the standard for judging ESA actions.

ESRA recognizes that we cannot recover species without providing incentives for both small and large landowners. ESRA provides incentives such as estate tax deferrals for lands enrolled in endangered species conservation agreements, tax credits for cost of implementing pro-active measures, and tax deductions for certain state and local property taxes for habitat managed under an agreement.

ESRA contains innovative new provisions that will give assurances to landowners while protecting species and taxpayers. ESRA allows permit holders to undertake activities that may damage habitat if they agree to mitigate those impacts, but provides them with assurances that they will not incur unforeseen mitigation costs in the future. In exchange, they file a performance bond that would cover the costs of the agreed to mitigation measures, ensuring taxpayers will not be left with the bill for mitigating these foreseeable adverse impacts of habitat destruction.

ESRA encourages ecosystem planning on a regional basis. ESRA encourages the development of multiple landowner, multi-species conservation plans. These plans would provide some surety to counties and other local governments that establish regional economic development plans, allow "one stop shopping" for permits, and enable groups of landowners to pool their performance bonds.

ESRA is supported by more than 300 environmental, religious, fishing, consumer, and scientific organizations representing millions of people across the country. Please consider becoming a co-sponsor when I reintroduce this balanced, workable legislation that is intended to achieve the goal the overwhelming majority of Americans support: recovery of endangered species.

Sincerely,

GEORGE MILLER
Senior Democratic Member

Source: House Resources Committee, at http://resourcescommittee. house.gov/105cong/democrat/dcjan25.html

July 23, 2002

Support our troops by cutting their taxes

Dear Colleague:

As America continues to wage war on terror, it is vitally important to remember the sacrifices that the men and women of our military make to protect our freedom and ensure our safety. I have introduced legislation, H.R. 4974, to compensate them for their tireless service to our country by exempting active duty members of the armed forces from federal income taxes.

Current law exempts members who serve directly in combat zones from federal income taxes, and my bill would extend that exemption to the entire active force. There are over 1.3 million men and women in our active force, who pay a staggering $2.5 billion in federal income taxes. These men and women deserve our support, both moral and financial. If you are interested in cosponsoring this bill, please contact me or my Legislative Director. . . .

Sincerely,

John Culberson
Member of Congress

Rank	Basic Pay	Federal Income Taxes
General	$138,200	**$27,176**
Colonel	$89,157	**$13,477**
Major	$60,803	**$6,644**
Captain	$48,344	**$5,089**
Sergeant	$23,709	**$1,042**
Corporal	$19,198	**$857**
Private	$14,872	**$609**

Source: Department of Defense Directorate of Compensation

Appendix III
Getting a Job
or Internship in
the Congress

Many students in political science hope one day to work on Capitol Hill. As you know, congressional staff serve many important functions. Staff at the entry levels ensure the smooth operation of the office. They transact much of the routine business and the constituency service that is the lifeblood of members' work and reelection campaigns. Staff members also monitor pending legislation, and many of them write legislation, determine legislative strategy, and even represent their elected bosses at important governmental functions. For these reasons, working on the Hill is exciting and fast paced. It can also be difficult to find a job out of college, in large part because Hill jobs often require previous experience in the form of an internship and/or a prior relationship with the person doing the hiring. In other words, getting a job on Capitol Hill requires good networking skills and—often—prior experience. For that reason, it's important to try to get experience before graduation in the form of an internship or summer job with a member's office. Internships can serve another important function as well; during the course of your internship on Capitol Hill, you might discover that you are simply not going to enjoy the high-pressure, fast-paced demands of working in the U.S. Congress.

If you are serious about getting an internship on the Hill, you will need to plan ahead. There are two main ways of tracking down an internship. The first is to pound the pavement. What this means is that you should start by contacting anyone you know who has a connection to Capitol Hill—a friend with an entry-level position, an uncle who lobbies on the Hill, or a neighbor who used to work for a senator, for example, could each likely put you in touch with someone in a position to offer you a job or internship. A lot of students worry about doing this. They don't want to get a job simply based on their connections, or they worry that asking a friend to talk to someone in her office about job openings will cause the chief of staff to think they are annoying. Wrong!

Anyone who has ever worked on Capitol Hill will tell you that networking is absolutely essential to getting a job or internship—and that the more you network, the better chance you'll have of finding a position. Although it certainly varies from office to office, the average tenure of an entry-level staffer is somewhere between six months and one year. That means that offices are always looking for talented people to hire at the entry level.

Pounding the pavement also means calling congressional offices, consulting their Web sites, and making "cold calls" to offices that may or may not be accepting internship applications. Most offices begin accepting applications for summer interns around the first of the year—by March, nearly all offices have accepted all the interns they plan to accept for the summer. In some cases, members' offices will even have accepted interns for the following summer. So, the bottom line is that the serious intern candidate has to be organized well in advance of the date he or she wishes to start working.

The second method of finding an internship is frequently more costly, but generally offers a better chance of finding an internship. This second method is to work through an established, credit-bearing Washington semester or Washington internship program.

With most Hill internships, do not expect to be paid for your efforts. Although a good intern is invaluable to a member of Congress and his or her congressional staff, there are literally thousands of prospective interns from whom members can choose. So, there are few internship opportunities that will provide compensation. Some offices will work with you to try to help you get course credit for the work you put in, but others won't. (That doesn't mean that your own institution doesn't have a provision to allow you to get credit—and you should look into that any time you decide to do an internship.)

Much of this same advice applies to the person who is looking for a job on the Hill. However, in the case of bona fide job openings, it does not make sense to apply for a job far in advance of when you will be available to start. It is standard for most staff members to give two weeks' notice that they are leaving. Give or take a day, this frequently means that the office wants someone to be able to start in two weeks or less. When you see a job listing, you should apply *as quickly as possible.* You should also be certain to follow the instructions in the advertisement. If the ad says "no phone calls," then don't call. If the ad says to include a writing sample, include a writing sample. Brief research or reaction papers or published articles (such as in a campus newspaper or journal of student writing) typically make fine writing samples.

Sometimes, the advertisement won't specify who the member of Congress is that is hiring; instead, it will simply say something to the effect of "Progressive northeastern Republican senator seeks . . ." This can be disconcerting, but it's fairly common. The reason these advertisements sometimes do not list the member is that some members have reputations—good or bad—that might make people more or less likely to apply for the position. For example, an advertisement that says "Liberal New England Democrat seeks . . ." would be more likely to yield applicants who are sincere in their ideological beliefs, whereas "Senator Ted Kennedy seeks . . ." might yield a whole host of applicants who are neither interested in nor qualified for the position, but who simply want to work for Senator Kennedy.

The types of jobs that you will likely be qualified for as a recent college graduate (with or without prior internship experience) have titles such as "staff assistant," "legislative correspondent," or "constituency relations specialist."

These are considered entry level, and are a good way to get your foot in the door on the Hill. Keep in mind, however, that these jobs frequently have starting salaries in the low- to mid-$20,000 range—so most entry-level staff must share housing with others in order to afford to live close to work.

Finally, whether you are applying for a job or an internship, you will want to be certain to approach offices in a professional manner. I've already explained that you should follow the directions listed in the position advertisement. In addition, you should dress appropriately for an interview. In fact, you should dress professionally even if all you are doing is dropping off resumes. You never know whom you might encounter when you walk through a congressional office's front door. In addition, never assume that the person sitting behind the desk is an intern—for all you know, it could be the office's chief of staff, even if he or she looks young, is dressed casually, and is sitting at the front desk. When I worked on the Hill, the chief counsel of a Senate Judiciary Committee subcommittee told me a story: She always took her interns with her to meetings, and in one case, the intern happened to be a man in his mid-30s. At a meeting with staff members from the White House Office of Legislative Affairs, the White House staffer walked in, looked at the two of them, and assumed that the intern (because he was older and male) was the chief counsel. The White House staff member barely glanced at the *real* chief counsel, who was actually responsible for making the decisions that the White House cared about. Needless to say, the staffer didn't get what he asked for during the meeting. The moral of the story, of course, is don't make assumptions. Treat everyone courteously and with respect.

The *Washington Post* offers the following additional suggestions about interviewing:

1. Do your homework. Be prepared and research the member of Congress or the committees that you're approaching. 2. Know your politics. It's important to know who represents your district, who your senators are, what happened in recent political campaigns, and what issues are important to your region and state. 3. Be open to a variety of positions and opportunities. A key goal is getting a foot in the door, so look at committees, congressional research organizations and internships. 4. Don't burn bridges during your job search. You'll be amazed who's up and down in one week in Washington.★

There are many, many opportunities to find internships and jobs on the Hill. It does take time and effort, however, and to that end, I've compiled a list of sources and resources that you might find helpful as you think about your future career plans. Some of these resources are in the form of job lines and government information hotlines. Others provide important information about how members' offices function. Not all of these are links for internships in the Congress itself; many government offices provide internships that are related to the Congress. Moreover, finding an internship or a job in the Congress can be difficult, so gaining experience through other Capitol Hill and government positions can be an excellent way to build your resume toward finding that job in the Congress.

★Krissah Williams, "Long Hours, Low Pay: The Thrill of It All: Job Seekers to Converge on Capitol Hill, Compete to Join Congressional Staffs," *Washington Post*, December 29, 2002, p. K1.

Employment Opportunities

Administrative Office of the U.S. Courts
Thurgood Marshall Building
Washington, DC 20544
Employment Opportunities List:
http://www.uscourts.gov/employment.html

Office of Personnel Management (Executive Branch Positions)
http://www.usajobs.opm.gov/
http://www.studentjobs.gov/index.htm

United States Department of Labor
Summer Internship Program
Intern Coordinator
200 Constitution Ave. NW, Room S-2235
Washington, DC 20210
Phone: 202-693-6490
Fax: 202-693-6146
http://www.dol.gov/_sec/media/internprogram.htm

U.S. House of Representatives
263 Cannon House Building
Washington, DC 20515
House Jobs Hotline: 202-225-2450
http://www.house.gov/cao-hr/

U.S. Senate
142 Hart Senate Office Building
Washington, DC 20510
Senate Jobs Hotline: 202-228-JOBS or 202-224-9167

U.S. Supreme Court
Judicial Internships/Fellowships
c/o Judicial Fellow, Administrative Assistant to the Chief Justice
Supreme Court of the United States, Room 5
Washington, DC 20543
202-479-3415

Semester-Long Internship Programs

The Washington Center
2301 M Street NW, Fifth Floor
Washington, DC 20037
http://www.twc.edu

American University
Washington Semester Program
4400 Massachusetts Avenue NW
Washington, DC 20016-8083
Toll-Free: 800-424-2600
Local: 202-895-4900
washsem@american.edu

Political Parties

Republican National Committee (RNC)
310 First Street SE
Washington, DC 20003
202-479-7000
http://www.rnc.org

Democratic National Committee
430 South Capitol Street SE
Washington, DC 20003
202-863-8000
http://www.democrats.org

United States Senate Republican Conference
405 Hart Senate Office Building
Washington, DC 20510
 202-224-2764
Online internship application at:
http://www.senate.gov/~src/about/intern/index.cfm

Senate Democratic Conference
The Democratic Conference serves three Democratic Leadership Offices,
each with its own internship program. The three programs can be contacted
separately at the addresses below, or prospective interns can fill out a single
electronic application at the following Web address:
http://democrats.senate.gov/intern_application.html

Democratic Policy Committee
Intern Coordinator
419 Hart Senate Office Building
United States Senate
Washington, DC 20510

Democratic Steering and Coordination Committee
Intern Coordinator
712 Hart Senate Office Building
United States Senate
Washington, DC 20510

Democratic Technology and Communications Committee
Intern Coordinator
619 Hart Senate Office Building
United States Senate
Washington, DC 20510

Dedicated DC Job/Internship Sites and
Newspaper Classified Advertisements

These classified listings include jobs not only inside the Congress but also in lobbying firms that work with the Congress.

Politixgroup.com
Publishes a monthly listing of jobs/internships available in Washington, DC, and in congressional districts and with election campaigns around the country.
http://www.politixgroup.com

Roll Call
(Capitol Hill newspaper)
Online at http://www.rollcall.com/classifieds

The Hill
(Capitol Hill newspaper—more conservative than *Roll Call*)
Online at http://www.thehill.com/classifieds/employment.shtm

The Washington Post
(major Washington, DC, newspaper)
Online at http://www.washingtonpost.com/wl/jobs/home

The Washington Times
(smaller DC newspaper—more conservative than the *Washington Post*)
Online at http://www.print2webcorp.com/news/washingtontimes/employmentextra/20021216/p1.asp

Index

CPSIA information can be obtained
at www.ICGtesting.com
Printed in the USA
FFOW01n1859080917
39742FF